The Coach's Toolbox

Using Sports Psychology
With
Your Kids

Dr. Peter S. Pierro, Ed.D.

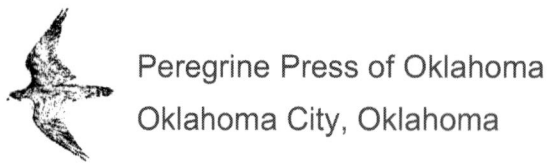

Peregrine Press of Oklahoma
Oklahoma City, Oklahoma

Printed in the United States of America

Copyright 2001, 2013 – Peter S. Pierro

Visit the author at www.peterpierro.com

All right reserved, which include the rights to reproduce this book in any form whatsoever except as provided under copyright Laws of the United States of America. Forms indicated in text may be reproduced for use in the training of players, parents, coaches, and other officials.

Book Design
40 Day Publishing
Oklahoma City, OK
www.40daypublishing.com

Books by Dr. Pierro

The Coach's Toolbox - Using Sports Psychology with Your Kids

There's Sports and there's Psychology and the two fit together very nicely. Dr. Pierro takes the ideas that we have discovered about how people learn and uses them to help kids play the game better and enjoy the game more.

Growing and Learning - Discovering your Child's Unique Learning Style

Growing and Learning is based on the idea that each of us learns in our own unique way, at our own special pace. Your child, and not the program, will be at the center of his learning experiences.

The Family Team - Parents, Coaches and the Kids Working Together

We Parents and Coaches are partners with our Kids in their sports ventures. The Game belongs to them and only to them and we are there to help them have great life experiences.

The Tyranny of Achievement Testing

You can help your child do better than simply survive in this world of Achievement testing - and you can help humanize our schools in the process.

About the Author – Dr. Peter S. Pierro

Dr. Pierro is a retired professor at the University of Oklahoma. He has degrees in history, psychology, and education from Northern Illinois University. He has also been on the faculty at Elmhurst College, Southeastern Oklahoma University, and Langston University.

Among other sports experiences, he played with the Will-Walt team in the Northern Illinois Fastball League, the Utica Yanks semi-professional baseball team, and U. S. Navy and Illinois Valley Community College basketball teams. He was selected on the All-Star team on the U. S. Navy Tinian Island Basketball Team. During his senior year at NIU he was individual bowling champion.

He has taught at the elementary, junior high school, high school, and university levels and has coached basketball, baseball, and softball at the child, youth, high school, and adult levels. He received the Professor of the Year Award at Elmhurst College in Illinois and is a member of the Illinois Valley Community College Hall of Fame. Playing golf is his major sports addiction at this time. Dr. Pierro is available for speaking engagements, consulting, and clinics.

About the Book

Much of this thinking and planning of this book was developed while I was acting as a consultant with the Amateur Softball Association. Working with Cindy Bristow, Director of the Junior Olympic VIP Coaches Program, I developed an eight tape program, The Coach: Leadership for Excellence and a training book, The Coach's Guide to Dealing with Parents and Problem Players.

About The Photographs

As I was writing this book, I began collecting photographs of kids, very young to high school ages, who were involved in various sports. The only two criteria I used were that the kids were enjoying The Game (whatever that game might be) and that the adults in the pictures were positively assisting the youngsters in those experiences. My thanks to those who assisted me in this:

Lisa Hall, Photographer, Oklahoma City,

OK Iceland Sports Center, Bethany, OK

Cathi and Bruce Nelson, Tennis Instructors, La Salle, IL

Margie Watters, Yearbook Editor, Brink Junior High School, Moore, OK

Students: Lunden Scott, Whitney Green, Linzi Crawford, and Lam Nguyen

Dale Watts, Editor, Smoke Signals, Oklahoma Soccer Association

Wendi and Kacie Jackson, Oklahoma City, OK

Jodi Berge, Bethany, OK

Contents

- The Pre-Game Meeting 15
  - About Sports Psychology 17
  - Psychology and Learning 18
  - The Important Elements 18
  - The Examples in the Book 18
  - Team and Individual 18
  - The Pursuit of Excellence 19
- Chapter 1 – The Basics 21
  - The Basic Purpose of This Book 23
  - The Basic Unit - The Team 23
  - All Members of the Team Must Work Together 24
  - The Other Basic Unit – The Player 25
  - A Basic Premise of This Book 26
  - The Coach is the Teacher 26
  - Coach Bruce and Carol 28
  - The Basic Performance Modes 28
  - The Practice Mode 28
  - The Game Mode 30
  - The Reinforcement Model 31
  - Negative Feedback 31
  - The Awareness Model 31
  - The Basic Types of Information 32
  - Instinctive Knowledge 32
  - Learned Knowledge 33
  - How Do We Do All Of This? 33

    The Minds...34
    The Conscious Mind..34
    The Subconscious Mind 35
    What's The Point Of All This?.....................................37
    Has the Lesson Taken? 38
    The Unlimits of The Brain...39
    In Sports..39
    The Bicameral Brain...41
    The Organizing Half...41
    The Creative Half 41
    Barriers and History...42
    The "Barrier" Myths – The Natural............................42
    The Real Tragedy 44
Chapter 2...47
The Player/Learner at Play 47
    The Habit Forming Strategies......................................49
    Eleven Strategies To Get There Faster 50
    Establishing New Habits 51
    Replacing Old Habits with New Ones........................51
    Extinguishing Old Habits 52
    Behavioral Habits 53
    Strategy #1 – Primacy and Recency 54
    Comments 55
    Other Sports Examples 56
    Strategy #2 – Focus and Triggers 57
    Keeping Mentally Focused...60

    Triggers 61
    Strategy #3 – Repetition 62
    Repetition and Focused Practice 63
    When Does Fatigue Enter In With Your Kids 64
    Other Sports 64
    Strategy #4 – Anchoring 66
    A Revisit with a Self Anchor 68
    A Process for You 69
    Having Time for Anchoring 70
    Strategy #5 – Acting As If 71
    Strategy #6 – Reinforcement/Feedback 75
    Strategy #7 – Awareness 78
    Strategy #8 – Self-Talk and Affirmations 81
    Strategy #9 – Visualization 87
    Strategy #10 – Achievement 93
    Winners and Losers 94
    Strategy #11 – Closure 96
Chapter 3 101
The Coach - A Professional Teacher 101
    The Coach – The Teacher 102
    There Are No *Tabula Rasas* Here 103
    Positive Expectancy 103
    The Illness Model 105
    And The Wellness Model 105
    "I Don't Know How To. . ." 106
    Positive Expectancy and Self-fulfilling Prophecy 107

A Real Self-Fulfiller 107
Readiness 109
The Laws of Readiness 110
A Variation on the Readiness Theme 111
Ready or Not – They Are Always Ready 112
To Cut or Not to Cut? 112
The Sneaky Cut 114
Stages of Development 115
Emotional Readiness 116
Recognizing Uniqueness 117
The Natural Way Is the Best Way 118
Learning Models 119
The Learning Modalities 120
Sandy's Models 121
Our Senses in Action 123
Motivating Yourself 123
The Motivating Coach 124

Chapter 4 Planning For Success 125
Players' Rights and Responsibilities 127
Winning Strategies 129
Goal Setting and Success 133
Players Rights and Responsibilities 133
The Team - Working and Playing Together 133
Team; a Set of Individuals with Common Goals 133
Goal Setting Principles 134
Setting Team Goals – The Process 134

Step 1. Positive Expectancy 135
Step 2. Creating the Goals 135
Step 3. Affirmation of Goals 136
Step 4. Motivating Your Players 136
Coaches are Teachers and Teachers are Coaches 139
Step 5. Goals Achieved and Success 139
Visualize Your Goals 140
Never Lose Sight of Your Major Goal 140
Positive Personal Goals 140
Winning and Competition 141
Winning 141
"Winning Isn't Everything." 142
I Played My Heart Out, Isn't That Good Enough? 144
"I'm A Winner." Really, in Everything You Do? 144
Who Wants To Be A Loser - Loser - Loser? 144
Competition 145
Fair and Honest Competition 145
Adjusting the Competition 145
Competition in Adults' Sports 146
Model #1 - The Big League Model 146
Model #2 - The Flight Model 146
Model #3 - The Handicapping Model 146
Model #4 - The Road Race Model. 147
Model #5 - The Special Olympics Model 147
Cooperation; the Partner of Competition 148
Praise and Encouragement 149

The Debriefing Meeting	154
Chapter 5	157
The Pack/Team Journals	157
The Team/Coach Agreement	160
Members of the Pack	160
PLAYER PROFILE	161
WHY I WANT TO PLAY	162
Player's Journal – Shared with your Coaches	163
PARENTS' INVENTORY	165
The Team/Parent Agreement	166
Members of the Pack	166
Recommended Books	169

The Pre-Game Meeting

About Sports Psychology

It was about my third year of teaching and first full year of coaching that I began to connect my sports life with my graduate college school life. I was working on my master's degree and I was studying and reading a lot of Educational Psychology (ed. psych.). I had what the Gestaltists would call a flash of insight and I saw how ed. psych. could help me coach my basketball, baseball, and softball teams.

We were studying attention, closure, awareness, reinforcement, readiness, etc. in class and I began to think about what this stuff would mean on the basketball court. This was back in the 1950s and the term sports psychology didn't exist. I recall one class session in a Physical Education course when I was sharing with my fellow students an article from a golf magazine and my use of it in my own golf game. The author (I don't recall his name) said that if you were trying to hit a shot over a tree that you should "see" the ball going over the tree and let that visual determine your stance and grip and then hit the ball. I told them that I tried it and it worked. I got a lot of funny looks and head shaking from the other class members.

Those were the days before Dwight Stones in high jumping, Jack Nicklaus in golf, the Mahre brothers in skiing, and others were using visualization. I'm sure that one of my bowling idols back in the 1940s and 1950s, Joe Norris of one of the great Detroit teams, used visualization but it was called "line bowling" as differentiated from "spot bowling."

Now, we know about many of the techniques and skills that comprise "Sports Psychology." This book is designed to tell you what some of those techniques are and how they can be used – especially those related to Learning Theory. You don't need a degree in psychology to use them. In fact, I hope you'll keep saying to yourself, "This is just good, common sense." There's Sports and there's Psychology and the two fit together very nicely.

Psychology and Learning

Learning is much more than changing what we do. In order to really learn something we must change our feelings, thoughts, and perceptions about what we are learning. I may decide to learn how to hit a right-to-left draw off the tee so that I can add a few yards to my drives. In order to do that, I must change my thoughts about my total game. I have been hitting a left-to-right fade for all of my golf life. Now I have to change my visualizing process, my placement for my next shot, and my picture of what a good drive looks like. When we teach kids something new or are installing different habits, we're changing a number of things and we have to be patient while the changes take place.

The Important Elements

There are only two important elements in the youth sports business; The Kids and The Game. I will capitalize those words much of the time throughout the book because they are proper nouns; they are the people and the operation in this business. Ordinarily, I use the male gender because he/she and other such terms are so clumsy. I'll use a lot of female coaches and players throughout the book.

The Examples in the Book

The skills and techniques of psychology and learning can be used in every sport. My sports experiences have been mainly in softball, bowling, baseball, basketball, and golf. I see best how things work in those sports and I, therefore, tend to write about and use them in my examples. I am working on including other sports as much as I can but I must leave much of the implementation of these sports psych things up to you tennis, volleyball, football, hockey, diving, gymnastic, and so on coaches.

Team and Individual

The materials in this book are for both the improvement of skills for individual players and for the development of better team operation. These two elements go together; they are inseparable; in team sports such as soccer, basketball, volleyball, football, hockey, etc. It's really a great experience watching a star athlete and team player at work. And it's great watching an excellent coach making this happen through her knowledge of the kids and the game. These people are winners regardless of the final score.

The Pursuit of Excellence

If, in fact, you can be a successful coach or player even though your team doesn't win every game or every title, there must be some goals that are higher than winning. We are not going to downgrade winning in this book. Having a choice between winning and losing, I'll take winning every time – I always hated to lose as a coach and as a player. Regardless of the circumstances, we have to help our youngsters learn all of the values of playing The Game.

There are two goals that exceed the goal of simply winning games – they are:

The pursuit of excellence.

The realizing of your potential.

Chapter 1 – The Basics

The Wolf and the Pack

Now this is the Law of the Jungle
As old and as true as the sky;
And the Wolf that shall keep it may prosper,
But the Wolf that shall break it must die.
As the creeper that girdles the tree trunk,
The Law runneth forward and back
For the strength of the Pack is the Wolf
And the strength of the Wolf is the Pack.

The Second Jungle Book
Rudyard Kipling

The Basics of Coaching/Teaching

The Basic Purpose of This Book

The basic purpose of this book is to take the ideas that we have discovered about how people learn and how they operate in this world and to use these ideas to help our kids play the game better and enjoy the game more. These ideas are universal—they're present in everything we learn—and they're present in all sports.

These ideas are not neatly lined up and sequential. In fact, the strength of them is that they interact and support one another. We may be dealing with Focus and then Visualization pops up to help illustrate what we're talking about. We will use practical activities as much as possible. Since this book is not about any particular sport, we will be using different sports as models at different times.

The Basic Unit - The Team

The concept of the Team throughout this book will be based on the Wolf and the Pack. I have been working with students, players, teams, and parents for all of my adult life and I have developed my own system, the one that works for me, and I've always had trouble describing it to other people - I knew what it was but I couldn't verbalize it. Then I ran across this marvelous book, entitled Sacred Hoops, written by Phil Jackson, former coach of my favorite team, the Chicago Bulls (I grew up in northern Illinois). In this book, Coach Jackson states his ideas about the team and the players and the connections between them. Of the many books I've read about leadership and motivation, this is the simplest and best. Anyway, it feels right for me. At the beginning, Coach Jackson quotes a poem entitled The Wolf and the Pack from the Second Jungle Book by Rudyard Kipling. That's a copy of it on the

The Basics

facing page. For this book The Pack consists of the Coaches, the Players, and the Parents.

All Members of the Team Must Work Together

As I understand the Law of the Jungle, the Pack is dependent on each individual Wolf and each individual Wolf is dependent on the Pack. The Pack consists of different kinds of wolves, each with his own unique talents; one is a great tracker, another is a speedster but tires after a short distance, another is a long distance runner who plods along but is there when needed, another is the one you want in the final battle, and so on. They all come together as a single, effective force— Coaches, Players, and Parents.

However, if a single Wolf goes off by himself he will die because he isn't capable of doing all of the necessary tasks, fulfilling all of the necessary roles needed to be successful. It is also true that if a single Wolf were to leave the Pack, it would suffer the loss of any skills or talents that Wolf brought to the group.

Your Team is dependent on each individual Player with her unique gifts and talents. Not everyone has the strong arm needed by the pitcher, not everyone has the speed to cover the entire area of center field, not everyone has the hands that can scoop up a sharp grounder and get it over to first before the runner gets there. On offense, you know the Player you want to be standing on second base with two outs in the final inning and you know who you would like to have at bat and they probably aren't the same Player. And, of course, each Player is in need of her Team. Only when the Team is at its best, can the Player really express her excellence. In a nutshell, our task as coaches is to make each individual player the best that he or she can become while having the team work together as an effective unit.

The Other Basic Unit – The Player

Sometimes we Coaches get so involved with what our team is doing that we forget that we are dealing with individual people. Each of our kids is a unique person who must be treated in a unique way. We have to deal with each of our Players in terms of where he is not where we want him to be or expect him to be. We deal with each of our Players in terms of how she performs not how we perform or what we believe to be the right way to perform. Sandy is a unique person and player and we'll treat her this way.

The Basics

A Basic Premise of This Book
The Coach is the Teacher

As the coach, you teach your players all the skills and strategies. That's your job – what we want to do is to help you help your players play the very best that they are capable of

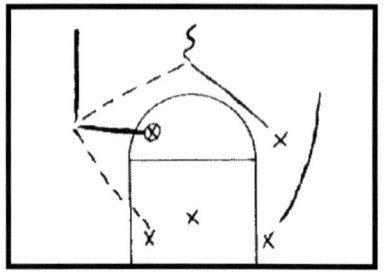

doing. Sandy has just joined the Cardinal basketball team whose offense is built on the fast break. Sandy is a very good guard but his previous team didn't fast break - Coach Haley needs to teach him what guards do on this play. He doesn't know that the guard on the side of the rebound is to clear himself for the outlet pass and the other guard is to take the center lane. Sandy is used to going to get the ball and bringing it up the floor.

What does Coach Haley do about it and how will he do it? He learns as much as he can about how Sandy learns and what he is capable of learning at his stage of development. Then, he may give him oral directions, he may draw him a diagram, he may demonstrate what he wants, he may walk him through it, he may have him visualize the process – or he may do several or all of the above. This is where we may be able to help you help your Sandys by sharing with you eleven strategies including; Focusing, Anchoring, and Visualizing. We will do a complete review of usage of those strategies in the section called Sandy and the Outlet Pass at the end of Chapter Two

A Semi-True Personal Story: For my birthday, I got a gift card for some golf lessons at any one of our really good community golf courses. Now, at my age, I'm not sure that I don't know more about my golf swing than I want to know. Is it "You can't teach an old dog new tricks" or "You're never too old to learn?" Anyway, I met Golf Pro Akers at the Lake Whitney Course and after we had exchanged some greetings, he dropped a ball, had me take out my

The Basics

six iron and said, "OK, line with the ball between your feet." Then he said, "Take the club back without breaking your wrists."

This went on with him telling me the "correct" way to stand, to move, and swing. After about 15 minutes, I put my six iron back in the bag, said "Thank you" and walked away leaving Golf Pro Akers wondering what had happened. I retrieved my gift card from the cashier and drove over to the Old Orchard Course.

Golf Pro Canale met me at the range. He told me to take out my six iron and he dropped some balls and said, "Hit 'em." After a few strokes, he said, "Take the club back on the inside a little bit." I did and it felt good. We went through some other clubs. Each time he had me hit a few and then made positive adjustments in my stance and swing. It was a good learning experience for me and I thanked Golf Pro Canale for his help.

G.P. Akers had the "correct" golf swing, the swing he had been taught to teach to everyone and was changing my swing to his "idealist" swing. G. P. Canale had me keep my natural swing and made adjustments, relative to that swing, so that I got better results.

The Basics

Well, here's Betty at her new sport. What are we going to do about that grip and stance? Maybe a lot – Maybe a little – Maybe nothing. We'll see.

Coach Bruce and Carol

I enjoy watching Coach Bruce working with very young tennis players. Carol is 6 years old and just starting her life experiences with the game of tennis (that's her on the Chapter 1 Title Page). Coach Bruce is her first coach. He's teaching her the fundamentals of the game, but first and foremost, he is teaching Carol, his student, how to be an independent player. He watches how she moves, how she swings, how she gets into position, and how she handles situations (good and bad). He gets to know who and what she is. He is constantly encouraging her and helping her improve herself.

"Turn your shoulders a little more." "Good move – swing right through the ball." Now she's standing on a line, shoulders perpendicular to the net with the racquet in a two-handed backhand grip ready to hit a ball being bounced to her. This is Fun!

The Basic Performance Modes

The Practice Mode

The purpose of the practice mode is to have the kids learn new skills and mechanics and to sharpen up the ones they have already learned. You can teach the skills and shorten Jessica's stride so she won't strike out so much – you can teach Gary how to make the backhand pickup at second base, etc. You can teach your players the rules and procedures of the game; the infield fly rule, tagging up after the catch before trying to advance, taking off for second on the pitch when the count is 3 and 2 with 2 outs, etc. You can teach your infielders the strategies that will be used in the games; infielders running down a runner, shortstop getting the relay from the center fielder, outfielders calling each other off to make the catch; etc.

The Practice Mode is also for you to improve yourself on a skill to the point that you will be able to perform when the time comes for the use of that skill. You're standing on the 12th tee, a par 4 hole with a dogleg to the left, and it simply is not the time and place to think about changing your grip so that you might be able to hit a hook around that big oak tree the way you saw that professional do it on TV. That kind of experimenting must be done on the practice tee (It also ends you up in the middle of the woods).

In a like manner, it simply doesn't make any sense to use a new tactic in a game situation that your players haven't had experiences with in the practice mode to the point of at least some degree of "automatic."

Situation: The winning run is on third with one out and Coach Eager thinks, "Wow, this would be a great time to work a suicide squeeze!" Ken, the batter, is a pretty good bunter and Ronnie is a good runner. His kids have been bunting for hits with some success. So he stops the game and tells his third base coach that he's going to have Ken lay down a bunt on the first base side on the first pitch and for Ronnie to take off on the pitch.

Now, Ken and Ronnie have never heard of this maneuver before. So they certainly haven't had any practice mode experiences. They have practiced bunting for a hit and that is tucked away in their memory banks.

Well, you know all of the things that might happen and 95% of them are not good for Coach Eager and his team. The most likely possibility happens. The pitch comes in high and inside. Ken has practiced diligently to bunt only pitches that are over the plate and his automatic system has him lay off the pitch – he hasn't practiced bunting a bad pitch to protect the runner. The opposing catcher is surprised to find Ronnie running up the line to get tagged out.

The Basics

The Game Mode

Bob Rotello in his excellent books on the mental side of golf calls this the Trusting Mode. You have to trust what you have learned in your practice session and then do it. The key word, of course, is trust - no second guessing. You have debated between hitting a 7 iron and an 8 iron to the green and you just selected the 8 iron. The 7 iron has just disappeared from your conscious mind - you're entire focus is on hitting that 8 iron as well as you can and you then must rely on your "automatic" skills. Sam Snead was once asked what he thought about as he was addressing the ball and he said, "If I thought about anything, I would probably miss the darn ball."

Rich (name changed to protect my friendship), a former member of my golf foursome, used to go through a whole list of swing checks every time he hit a ball. By the time he actually swung, he had talked himself out of making a good swing. We finally got him to check just one or two things and his natural swing took over and enabled him to hit better shots. As a result, he lowered his handicap quite a bit and we moved along a lot faster.

Let's get back to Coach Eager and the suicide squeeze:

Situation: After the last game, and the not-so-good experience with the suicide squeeze, Coach Eager thought about adding it to his team's storehouse of tactics and doing it correctly this time. His kids already have had practice experiences with bunting so all Coach has to do is to add some new skills and some understanding of how it fits into the game, how it is executed, and what things must be done with the suicide squeeze that were not included in bunting for a hit. Then practice, practice, practice, until it becomes "automatic."

When you have learned a new skill in the Practice Mode, you must trust yourself and use it without fear in the Game Mode.

You will use both a reinforcement model and an awareness model so that your players will learn their skills until they become "automatic" - without "thinking."

The Reinforcement Model

The reinforcement model is very simple to use - in fact, we all use it all the time with our children, our pets, our employees, our friends. When someone does something that you like, you are apt to give him a verbal reward, "Thank you, I really appreciate that." Your positive response will tend to make him happy, he will be reinforced on his good work, and be more inclined to repeat it. We most often don't realize that we're using it. We usually use it honestly and responsibly (but it can be used dishonestly and irresponsibly). This is very effective model in building mechanical skills and common types of behavior.

Negative Feedback

Let's be careful that we don't use this very effective technique in a negative way. Remember when you were working with Fido and he didn't sit when you told him to; you didn't yell, "You stupid dog, what's wrong with you? Can't you learn anything?" Believe it or not, I've heard coaches and parents make those kinds of comments to their players/kids right out in public in front of friends, spectators, teammates, strangers, and other interested parties. Hard to believe, isn't it?

So, what happens to your pitcher when you holler at him for not backing up the catcher on a throw to the plate? Does he really bear down on the next batter? Where is his mind?

The Awareness Model

I'm sure you recognize some basic Gestalt concepts:

The whole is more than the sum of the parts.

The Basics

Your team is more than a bunch of players. It also includes all of the interactions of these players. The team works as a unit, not as a bunch of individuals.

The whole is affected by each of its parts.

The actions and/or presence of each of the players affects the whole team. We, in Oklahoma, were very aware of this during the 2009 football season when our Heisman Trophy winning quarterback, Sam Bradford, got hurt early in the season.

Did you ever have a guard on your basketball team who was aware of "the whole floor" or a quarterback in football who could "see the whole field?" You may be lucky enough to have that soccer player who knows where all of his teammates and opposing players are even as he is focusing on the ball and going for the goal." These players can make much better use of their skills because they are aware of how these skills are to be used. Have your kids get involved in the whole game so they can use their skills and knowledge correctly and effectively.

In Chapter 2, #7 Awareness, we will be demonstrating how this works in practice and game situations.

The Basic Types of Information

Instinctive Knowledge

Sometimes we think that the kids learn this game instinctively – Not so. Instinctive behavior is putting your glove up in front of your face when the ball is heading for your nose. You don't teach that. It's not instinctive behavior for little Donna to hit the ball off the tee and head for first base. It would make as much sense at this stage in her development for her to head for third base or the pitcher's mound or to her Mom and Dad in the bleachers.

The Basics

Learned Knowledge

Dan is learning the correct skills, mechanics, procedures, strategies, and rules in order to play soccer well – to the best of his ability with the assistance of Coach McGahey.

That's what we call "Coaching." Coach McGahey is setting the conditions, teaching the skills, and giving the necessary information so that Don learns how to play the game as well as he is capable of playing. Another way of stating what we do is to have our players become so proficient with the Learned Knowledge and Skills that they begin using them "Instinctively."

How Do We Do All Of This?

What can I do with the mental side of the game to improve the physical and mechanical sides of the performance of my players? How can I help my players perform consistently at the level they are capable of performing? That's what this book is all about.

The Minds

We want our players to learn the tactics and strategies of the game so well that they'll know what to do and when to do it. That's the job of the Conscious Mind.

We also want our players to learn their skills so well that they won't have to think about them as they're playing - they'll know how to do them and then just do them. That's the job of the Subconscious Mind.

This means that we'll work with them in the Conscious Mind (during the practice) so that these skills will be carried out in the Subconscious Mind (during the performance) - to become 'automatic' so that they will be done without having to think about it. We will also work with them so that they know the game so well they will be able to "think on the run" and be able to make the correct moves.

We will also be aware of and make usage of the different functions of the two parts of the brain so that our players will develop organization and decision-making skills.

The Conscious Mind

The conscious mind deals with new things, new thoughts, new ideas, new decisions. As you are reading this your conscious mind is absorbing the information and deciding what to do with it. It may choose to reinterpret it in terms of your knowledge and/or beliefs about this topic; it may reject it totally and refuse it add it to your data base; or it may find it interesting and add it to your present knowledge and reaccess and revise that knowledge.

When you're teaching your kids new strategies and skills, you're working with them in the conscious mode. You know they need to have new information added to the information that they now have. You have to expect them to have some difficulties because this is new stuff. Mistakes will be a part of the process. You should look for the simplest ways to help your players get better.

The players have to understand that any new skill they learn will feel "unnatural" for a while. When you have Allie bring the ball up from hip level to eye level to shoot her free throws, she's going to say, "That feels funny." It does feel funny because you are taking her out of her comfort zone. A few weeks later if you told her to try a free shot from hip level, she would say, "That feels funny." That change has gone from the conscious to the subconscious level and we can call it habitual behavior.

Practicing in the conscious mode must be very focused. For example, you have just told Allie to take 25 shots with her new position. She is very focused for 10 shots and then she starts getting careless and sloppy - the last 7 or 8 shots are just thrown up there. In this case, practice is actually worse than no practice. She is now building a poor action into her performance and it will erase and replace her good work. I believe that a lot of coaches have the kids make too many repetitions of a skill. I deal more with this in the section of Repetition in Chapter 2.

The Subconscious Mind

The subconscious mind runs about 90% of our lives. It has to do with the common, everyday things that we do such as turning the key the correct way to unlock our door. We don't "think" or have to make a decision about whether to turn to the left or to the right every time we unlock a door. It's done "automatically" without conscious thought. And what a great benefit that is to us. Just imagine if we had to make a decision or choose an option every time we reached for our toothbrush, tied our shoes, or started our car.

The Basics

We lump all of these kinds of decisions into something called "habits." I have just gotten up in the morning and I'm not operating very efficiently. I go to the bathroom sink and I turn the knob to the left of the faucet counter-clockwise and wait for the water to warm up. I pick the soap up from the soap dish which is in its usual place to the right of the sink. I turn the cold water knob counter clockwise and adjust the two knobs so that I get the temperature I want for washing my face. I pick up my washcloth from the rack - And, thankfully, I have not had to make a single decision.

Now how would it be if I had to use my conscious mind. Just think what it would be like if you had to make these kinds of decisions on every occurrence. I'm still half asleep and I'm standing at my bathroom sink. Now, which knob is for the hot water? Oh, yes, it's the one with the "H" on it. And, now, which way do I turn it? I simply turn to the left and it works. When I was visiting in England, sometimes I had to try different things until I got the desired effect. This is called trial and error and is a very hard, wasteful, sometime hurtful, way to learn.

Situation: I've just landed at O'Hare Field in Chicago and I'm picking up my rental car. The clerk gives me the ignition key and I get in the car – ready to go. I have no trouble finding the lock (same place as in my car) and I insert the key. Let's see, do I turn the key to the left or to the right? A no-brainer (literally, a no-brainer because I don't have to think or decide), I turn the key to the right and go on from there doing the "automatic", "habitual" things, such as putting on my seat belt, putting the lever into reverse to back up, stepping on the gas, turning the wheel to the left, stepping on the brake, putting the lever into drive, and all of the other things I normally do.

The subconscious mind is doing well for us. However, after driving for a while it starts getting dark and I need to turn on my head lights. Oh, oh! The light switch in my car is on the left steering column lever. I just twisted this one and the windshield wipers showed that they work. Now, I have to think and my conscious mind takes over – where could the switch be?

It could be on the dashboard and there it is – the dial on the left side. So I reach out and turn it– to the right, of course. The subconscious mind is working well. We are using our old skills and knowledge to supplement the decisions we have to make with this new situation and we're doing very well.

Sports Situation: You are 9 years old and playing shortstop – nobody on base – grounder hit slightly to your right. Decisions to be made: Do I get in front of it or stay on the side? What do I do with it if and when I pick it up? Who do I throw it to? Do I throw it at all? It might hurt my hand, so maybe I shouldn't try to get it, or maybe it will be OK – what should I do?

Now, if you are a nine year old, those questions will make sense to you because you are dealing with a new situation and you have to think about it and make decisions. Children don't have all that stuff stashed away in their sub-conscious minds yet. They need to have experiences (good experiences) with recognition and reinforcement to build up their data bases.

For us adults, this play depends on how hard the ball is hit, whether we're fielding it shallow or deep, whether the runner on third is going in or holding or whether you're going to your left or right or if the ball is hit directly at you. But we veteran ballplayers have done this many, many times and we let the conscious mind work with it – gathering data and making a decision. In the meantime, your subconscious mind is fielding the ball.

What's The Point Of All This?

As coaches we have to deal with both the conscious thoughts and the subconscious actions of our players. In terms of the conscious mind, we must have our kids learn the rules, be aware of the correct actions to take in a given situation, learn more options that can be taken, then make good decisions. We

The Basics

want them to think! And but that thinking has to be based on good learning.

In terms of the subconscious mind, we must have our kids learn the right skills and actions – to learn how to swing the bat correctly, to learn how to pitch the rise ball, to make the double play pivot correctly, etc. We want them to get to the place where they do the mechanical, skills stuff correctly without thinking.

(Note: "Correctly" in this context means the way that you want them to operate. If I get your players next year, my correct way may be different from yours and the players will have to unlearn the old skills or procedures and relearn a new set of "correct" actions.)

Has the Lesson Taken?

You teach your kids to shoot free throws with their toes up to the line and the ball at eye level. Remember Allie has been making the change from her old style of shooting from the hip which was very ineffective, clumsy, and not done in a way that was natural for her. You've been watching her in practice and feel that she has mastered the new shot.

Happening: It's been a tight game and Allie is at the free throw line with a chance to tie the game. You see that she has taken a stance with the ball at hip level and she shoots from there.

Observation: Allie hasn't completely made the change a habit yet. She is not shooting from the eyes at the subconscious, automatic level.

Message to the Coach: When a player reverts to an old habit, she hasn't mastered the new skill and she needs to spend more time on it in practice – to move it into her playing mode. Don't yell "Eye level, Allie" – at this time her subconscious has more faith in the old shot than in the new one and your advice might confuse her. It needs more practice.

The Unlimits of The Brain

In talking about the mental side of playing and coaching, we need to deal with the Brain and the Mind. I bought a new DVD player recently and they gave me an owner/operator manual. I can make it work if I follow the directions. I was born with a Mind/Brain but I was never given an owner/operator manual so I had to learn as much as I could about how it works and I believe I have at least 2% of it under control.

The brain consists of 3 to 3½ lbs. of fatty tissue. It has a fantastic amount of storage space. It has the power to adapt, it can think, it can learn, it can visualize, it can have and express feelings, it can handle the complexities of language, it can make decisions, it can be creative, and it is conscious of its existence. Cogito ergo sum!

We sometimes make use of the computer as a metaphor for our mind but if you have ever stored a picture or complex design, you know how much storage space you need. Just think then of the amount of space needed to store all of the events of your day so far. Your thoughts, actions, and feelings for just a small fraction of your entire life. Then think of one of your most memorable sports experiences and bring it up. How much space was used to store all of that away, waiting for you to bring it up if you so choose? And after thinking about it, you send it back into storage to be brought up whenever you choose to use it again.

In Sports

You are playing center field – the ball is hit to your right and long. Your brain gathers some information; the sound of the bat on the ball, your eyes tracking the ball so that your brain can calculate the speed at which the ball is traveling and the height of the trajectory. Already in your brain there is the knowledge that the ball will take a parabolic path; it computes the speed at which you will need to run and the direction you

The Basics

must take and it charts the exact point to the fraction of an inch where the path of the ball and the pocket of your glove will intersect – Nice Catch!

In the same way, you have a bat in your hand, the pitcher is throwing a curve ball breaking away from you, you're swinging the bat so that the ball and the bat intersect the way you planned it, and the ball goes on a line into right center field.

When you think about a basketball player burying a three pointer; the center timing his jump so that his hand intercepts the flight of a shot; the soccer player, who on the dead run places the exactly correct part of his shoe on the exactly correct place on the ball so that it flies above the outstretched arms of the goalie and nestles into the upper right hand corner of the net; or the mental power and kinesthetic/tactile control of the ball by a quarterback as he figures how far to lead his receiver who is on the dead run fifty yards down field and lays the ball over his shoulder and into his hands, you can appreciate the power of your brain.

We can go on with many other sports related examples but before we deal with the barriers that we put up, let's mention just a few of the stretches of the mind that we know about so that we can ask the questions, "What are limitations?" "Are they real limitations or are they barriers that I put up myself?"

For example, Arturo Toscanini, the great conductor of the Metropolitan Opera had hundreds of operas, concertos, and other musical compositions in his memory banks and conducted without a score. It is recorded in chess annals that Harry Pillsbury, the American champion of the early 20th century, could recall every move that he and his opponent made in every game that he had ever played. And there's Einstein and Edison and . . .

Were their brains that much better than Eddie's, your defensive left tackle, who you're working diligently with so that he learns how to move correctly on that stunt and doesn't keep running into your left end? Probably. Were they using their brains more effectively? Probably. If that's true, then isn't it possible for us (and Eddie) to use our brains more effectively and improve our status? I hope so.

The Bicameral Brain

We all have this marvelous bicameral brain – the organized left hemisphere and the creative right hemisphere. They have different functions and we can use our information to help our players learn quicker and better.

The Organizing Half

The left hemisphere is concerned with structure, time, and sequence. We have our kids learn the rules and mechanics in this area by repetition, rote learning, practicing skills.

The Creative Half

The right hemisphere is concerned with creativity and possibilities. We have our kids learn tactics and strategies in this area by thinking about the situation, considering the possibilities, choosing the right option, making the right decision.

The two hemispheres can work together or separately – the goal is to have both hemispheres working together.

The Basics

Barriers and History
The "Barrier" Myths – The Natural

In the past, we have allowed and been restricted by natural barriers in sports achievement. There was the 4 minute mile, the 7 ft. high jump, the 60 foot shot put, and the 28 ft. long jump. I recall movie news spots on Glenn Cunningham of Kansas in the 1930s as he cut his time in the indoor mile finally to 4:04.4 minutes. In the 1940s, the Finns, Gunder

Haegg and Arne Andersson took turns reducing the outdoor time to 4:01.4 minutes. And then in May of 1954, Roger Bannister of England broke the barrier with a run of 3:59.4 minutes and all of a sudden runners from all over the world, including a high school Kansan by the name of Jim Ryun, were snipping seconds off the record. The current record is 3:43.13 minutes.

In 1956, Charles Dumas of the U. S. broke the 7 foot high jump barrier – the current record is 7 feet 11.5 inches. In 1952, Randy Matson of the U. S. broke the 60 foot shot put barrier – the current record is 75 feet 10.25 inches. At the 1968 Olympics in Mexico City, Bob Beamon not only broke the 28 foot long jump barrier – he sailed an unbelievable 29 feet 2 inches – the current record is 29 feet 4.5 inches. All of those old marks have fallen and strangely we don't deal with barriers very much any more – that's History.

Why is that? Because we have learned more about how the brain works, more about motivation, more about setting goals, and we no longer restrict our thinking about reaching new goals. Athletes began to realize that the only limitations we have are those we set for ourselves or we allow others to set for us. Presently, there is very little talk about limits with top amateur and professional athletes.

We're seeing faster track record, longer field records, quadruple jumps in figure skating, below 60 rounds in golf (59s by Sammy Snead, Al Geiberger, David Duval, and Annika Sorrenstam) – all demonstrating that barriers are in our heads. If our brain can conceive that something can be done; it can be done.

At the 1928 Olympics women were allowed to compete in longer track events for the first time; however, so many of them seemed to collapse (they really didn't) at the end of the 880-meter race that the event was banned until 1960. It was determined that their fragile bodies could not deal with races of that length. So, how are they doing now in the marathon?

Lately, we have been enjoying watching our granddaughter, Adrienne, competing in triathlons.

Deleting the Limitations

Let's return to the questions posed above, "What are limitations?" "Are they real limitations to my performance or are they barriers that I put up myself?" We don't know what Robby's limitations are. He is only 12 years old. Maybe if we don't tell him that he has limitations and don't keep reminding him what those limitations are, he just might become a lot better player than we think he can be.

The Real Tragedy

The real tragedy occurs when Robby has heard all those messages about him not being able to play and he says, "I guess they're right – I just don't have what it takes." The message has gone from what he can't do on the rink or field to what a poor example he is as a person.

> **Danger**! The message for Robby has gone from **what he does** as a player to **who he is** as a person.

The Basics

Chapter 2
The Player/Learner at Play

The Player's Learning/Habit Forming Strategies

These techniques are not separate from one another. In fact, as you use one of them, it is natural for others to pop up to carry on the process.

1. Primacy and Recency – The first time and the latest time that you do something are the most important.
2. Focus and Triggers – Keeping focused on reaching your goal will keep distractions from interfering with your performance.
3. Repetition – Practicing right makes perfect performance.
4. Anchoring – Storing your best performances so that you can bring them up when you want to improve your present performance.
5. Acting as if ... – Having your actions change your attitudes and beliefs about yourself.
6. Reinforcement – Using the basic reward system to maintain your progress.
7. Awareness – Knowing and using the whole picture.
8. Self-Talk and Affirmations – Using positive self-messages to achieve your goals.
9. Visualization – Using your "mind's eye" to speed up your progress.
10. Achievement – Reaching the goals that you set for yourself.
11. Closure – Completing tasks so that you can move on to new ones.
12. The whole is more than the sum of the parts. All elements interact with and affect each other. Each part affects the whole.

The Habit Forming Strategies

In this chapter we will be having our players learn new skills and improving on old skills. We'll be using the Falcons youth, co-ed softball team, to present each strategy. Then we'll deal with other sports and even come up with some ideas that you can use to make your life a little easier.

These techniques act in relation to each other and to the tools in the box below. We're going to put Head coach Cindy Doakes and assistant coaches Sara Garcia, and Glen Ames to work teaching our Falcon players while you and I look on. During this teaching/learning time the coaches want the players to be adept at and comfortable with this skill in the Practice Mode so that they will be able to use it correctly, without thinking, in the Game Mode.

We have at our disposal many techniques and we will be dealing with the eleven shown on the facing page. None of these is better than the others; each of them is simply more appropriate relative to the learners and to the skills or knowledge that are to be learned. You don't teach your 7 year olds the full court zone press regardless of how good a coach you are and how much command you have of your coaching skills.

In a like manner, you don't walk a college level player around the bases so that she knows you go from second to third and third to home. Yes, I know you have some "advanced" players that you sometimes feel that you have to get back to that level.

In addition, we have a set of teaching tools available:

Tools in the Toolbox

Oral Direction	**Demonstration**
Player Experience	**Visual Diagram**
Simulation	**Affirmation**
Praise	**Encouragement**

The Learner at Play

Generally in our coaching we should go from the concrete thinking, experiential approach to the abstract thinking, verbal approach. In the meantime, we mix in a lot of other good stuff even if we don't know how well based or how sound what we are doing really is.

Eleven Strategies To Get There Faster

We'll look at the eleven strategies that can help us teach our kids how to play better. They're not separated from each other – they'll flow together in a very natural way. You'll be asking a player to Focus (#2) on a task and find yourself giving a verbal reward Reinforcing (#6) his good performance.

In Chapter 1, we talked about the Conscious and Subconscious minds and the point was made that what we do in coaching to a great extent is to move our thinking from the Conscious to the Subconscious mind so that we can improve our performance on the field. In its simplest form, we try to have our players "get into the habit" of doing the right things on the field. We want them to tag second base while going from first to third without thinking "I have to tag second base." That skill will have been burned into the player's operation so that he can concentrate on picking up the signs from the third base coach.

Habits (from the Subconscious Mind) control 80 to 90% of our daily operation. The same thing is true in our playing sports. We need to act without thinking; to act 'instinctively' or 'automatically' or "by habit" most of the time. We need to program our game so that we make the right moves in action while we're using our minds to deal with the current situation. There are three issues to deal with on habit forming;

- **The establishing of new habits (Learning)**
- **The extinguishing of old unwanted habits (Unlearning)**
- **The replacing of old habits with new ones (Relearning)**

Establishing New Habits

Working with young players, the Falcons' coaches, Cindy Doakes, Glen Ames, and Sara Garcia are mainly concerned with establishing new habits. Larry Johnson came to the Falcons with no playing experience. When Coach Garcia works with him on fielding a ground ball in the outfield, she can go directly to showing him how to hurry to get in front of the ball, to get into the correct fielding position, to have him get his glove in the correct position, and so on. This is relatively easy because there are no old habits to unlearn as the new ones are acquired.

Replacing Old Habits with New Ones

However, Connie's case is much tougher. She has been coached by her parents from year one and she has acquired some "skills" that are keeping her from improving. Her dad wanted her to be a pitcher (What else?) so she would be the star. He had been a good baseball player but he knew nothing about underhand pitching. Connie learned a lot of poor habits especially in coordinating her arm swing with her stride. Coach Doakes has her playing third base while Coach Ames gives her pitching instruction.

In this case, the player has to replace some old, fairly well ingrained habits with new ones. One of the early problems that becomes very evident is the tendency of the player to revert back to the old ways when there's a critical situation.

Later in the Season

When Coach Ames had Connie Pearson pretty well coordinated on the mound, Coach Doakes decided to let her start a game at pitcher. She was doing pretty well but in the 3rd inning after an error in the infield and losing a hitter on a pretty good 3 and 2 pitch, she lost her cool and threw four balls to the next batter that didn't come near the strike zone.

The Learner at Play

Coach Ames jumps up in the dugout and says to Coach Doakes, "Get her out of there." Coach Doakes, "What did you see?" "She's back to her old arm swing and stride. She won't get another pitch over the plate." Coach Doakes having confidence in her assistant coach calls time and goes out to the mound to make the change.

When things went astray, Connie subconsciously reverted to her old, tried and trusted pitching style. This is often called "The Comfort Zone." Next practice, Coach Ames will be working again with Connie in the Practice Mode until she is really ready to trust the new pitching style and skills enough to stay with them in the Game Mode. She also needs some work on focusing.

We tend to revert to our old and comfortable ways when the situation gets critical.

Extinguishing Old Habits

Extinguishing old habits can be a bigger problem because you're asking someone to create a vacuum in his behavior –

The Learner at Play

vacuums invite old behaviors to come back. I had an experience with this when I left Langston University and took a position at the University of Oklahoma. In getting to Langston University, I used to travel north on I-35 and get off at the Guthrie exit. Several months later, I was going north on I-35 headed for Stillwater which is a good distance north of Guthrie.

Well, you know what happened – there I was on the off ramp at the Guthrie exit. I just laughed (there are times that we simply must laugh at ourselves), crossed over to the on ramp to I-35, and continued on my way. The next time, I traveled that way, I filled the vacuum by giving myself a verbal, visual cue and kept going north on I-35.

Behavioral Habits

Coach Doakes is concerned about the behavior of Clara (the Clown). One of her favorite antics is getting her teammate's attention as he steps into the batter's box and trying to make him laugh – funny faces, funny names, funny actions. It is fun and she gets a lot of positive feedback from the players who laugh along with her but it is distracting to the player who is trying to concentrate – to get the sign – to be ready for the pitch. Let's listen in to Coach Doakes as he tries to deal with this one:

Coach: Clara, what are you doing?

Clara: I'm helping take the pressure off Benny. He's too uptight.

Coach: When you're getting ready to bat, you close your eyes and do some deep breathing.

Clara: Yeah, Coach Garcia has been showing us how to focus better.

Coach: And how does it work for you?

Clara: It's great. I'm hitting a lot better now.

Coach: Now tell me how making Benny laugh helps him to focus.

The Learner at Play

Clara: Hmm. I never thought about that. But I've always done this fun stuff.

Coach: I know and you really have helped all of us enjoy the game more. But, is this the right time to do that with Benny?

Clara: I guess not – but I'm so used to doing things...

Coach: Will you do this for your team mates? Just ask yourself this question when you're having fun – how is this helping Benny and helping the team?

Clara: O. K. It's a deal – and I suppose you'll remind me. Coach: Of course, that's what coaches do.

Good habit change is not focused on what you did wrong – it deals with what you're going to do to make it right.

Strategy #1 – Primacy and Recency

The first time and the latest time that you do something are the most important.

The Falcons at Play

Primacy – The players have straggled into the park. They grabbed balls out of the equipment bags and started loosening up, playing catch. Coach Ames calls all of the infielders onto the diamond and is hitting easy grounders to them. They are coached to use good starting positions, getting in front of the ball, and throwing strikes to first base. Coach Garcia is out on the infield giving a lot of strokes, "Good pickup, Ollie." Parent helper, Geno Pacetti, is hitting nice, soft fly balls directly to the outfielders.

Recency – The players are practicing sacrifice bunting. Each one takes about 5 pitches. Paula has laid down three good bunts. On the third bunt, Coach Ames says, "Great job, Paula. Lay down another and run it out. "Larry is having trouble so Coach Ames says, "Try it again and this time get into the bunting stance sooner. Keep that bat level. "Larry lays down a good one on the seventh try and Coach Ames says, "Great job, Larry. Run that one out."

Practice comes to a close. The players sit in a semi-circle facing Coach Doakes who is concluding her wrap up, "Guys, we've had a good practice. Lots of hustle, lots of focus, lots of good teamwork. We're ready to take on the Comets tomorrow. Have a good night's sleep and be at Hegeler Park by 6:30 tomorrow night. Remember neat, clean uniforms and shined shoes."

Comments

It's important that the first experiences in a practice session are good, successful ones. That's why we warm up with easy grounders and then build up to tough ones. If we start out hitting scorchers at them they will have some pretty poor experiences to build on. In the bunting session, the player should take a successful attempt away with him. Coach Ames reinforced their good attempts with verbal rewards and sent the satisfied players on to their next task.

We store away the final part of an experience with our feelings. Feelings are more important than thoughts here. Let's say that Pablo Ruiz of the Chargers had played a good game but the coaches sent him and his teammates home after a thorough chewing-out for being sloppy on the base paths. Pablo's dad is waiting to pick him up and as Pablo opens the car door, Dad says, "Great game, Son" and Pablo says, "Humph." The Falcon's Head Coach Doakes won't let that happen – she is sending them home happy. The last experience of the game or practice is not the time to chew them out and have them take their hurt feelings home to sit on until the next game or practice. Also, parents will appreciate having happy kids come to their cars ready to go home.

There are so many examples of the use of this strategy without being aware of its use. Every salesman knows that you make a great first impression. And you may be sure that he will have you smiling when you leave. Movie people grab you right at the start and then send you home with something to keep it in your memory banks. They want you to remember it so well that you'll tell your friends about this good movie. If you attend a choral presentation here in Oklahoma, you will be sent home with a rousing rendition of "Oklahoma" and you will leave the theater humming it. (In the trade, this is called a "hummer.")

The Learner at Play

Notice how the cast is presented in movies and TV shows – how the producers deal with the ego of two super stars in the same film. They list one of them first, then after going through the lesser actors, they present the other star (usually adding, "As _____), and then they move on to something entirely different.

"If I can't be first, I want to be last – in fact, now that I think about it – I want to be last."

Other Sports Examples

When I get out to the driving range, I go through all of my clubs starting with the wedges and finishing with the driver. I hit each club about 6-8 times and I have to finish with a good shot before I go on. I won't put a club back into my bag without feeling good about it. This means that when I pull my 7 iron out on the course, I will have confidence in hitting it. After all, my latest experience with it left me feeling good.

I finish my practice with the driver because my next round of golf will be played at the Brookside Golf Course and the first hole is a par 4, dogleg right, 306 yard hole. I will visualize that hole and hit some drives out to the left center of the fairway to open up the hole for my approach shot. When I've hit a good drive, I'll anchor it and move to the practice putting green.

In tennis, you would want your players to start off returning easy serves and build up from there. Later, Cathi has been hitting some good practice serves and she has just stroked a beauty. Coach Bruce will anchor it by saying, "Fantastic, get over with the guys working on their backhands." Success breeds success.

Strategy #2 – Focus and Triggers

Keeping focused on reaching your goal and not allowing distractions to interfere with your performance.

The Falcons at Play

It's the bottom of the 7th and Coach Ames is saying to the Falcons as they're going out on the field to protect their 2 run lead. "Remember what we're doing. We need to focus on getting them out and closing out the game. Stay sharp!" Stan has pitched a good game but he got into a little skirmish with the other team last inning when he hit a homer and trotted just a bit slowly to nail down his accomplishment for the folks in the stands. The Bearcats got on him for his attitude and now the 1st and 3rd base coaches are laying it on him. "Stan the Showboat." "Hold that pose so I can take your picture." etc.

Stan has just walked a batter. He steps off the mound and Coach Doakes hears him say to the 3rd base coach, "Yeah? Look at the scoreboard. Who's winning?" Coach Doakes calls time and almost runs out to the mound. Let's listen in: "What's our goal, Stan? What did Coach Ames tell you and the team?"

"To stay sharp and focus on getting them out."

"Right, that's our goal. Now what is the goal of the Bearcats' coaches?"

"To beat us."

"Right. And now they're trying to get your attention off your job so you'll mess up." "Yeah, but I'll show 'em."

"Now, listen to me carefully. Stan, and I need an answer to this question? Are going to help them reach their goal or are you going to help us reach our goal?"

"Hey, I'm doing OK. I'll get 'em out."

That's not good enough. If you want to stay in the game, you'll have to tell me where your focus is going to be – on talking with them or on and getting them out."

"I'm going to focus on getting them out."

The Learner at Play

"O.K., Ignore them totally – they don't exist as far as you're concerned."

Coach Garcia comes back to the dugout and watches Stan carefully. If she sees one sign of Stan communicating with the other team, Connie takes the mound. Fortunately, Stan got the message and regained his focus. The whole idea of 'getting on a player' is to have him lose his focus. If he has "rabbit ears' it makes it easy to do that. You have to keep reminding your players to keep focused on their goals and the team's goals.

Our senses and perceptions have to be as focused as is our thinking.

Focus is a total and unified operation. Your thoughts, feelings, and actions must be coordinated on the task and on your goals. You are focused on the target whether that target is a goal that you have in your mind or a goal that you're trying to kick a ball into.

What makes a person or a team tough-minded? I believe that there are two important elements that are involved; focus and goal attainment. When a person or team is totally focused, that is mentally and physically focused, on the end result of the game, the ongoing strategies and plays, and even the play that is about to be run, they are going to operate with a great deal of effectiveness. If their opponent is not as focused, they are at a real disadvantage. When we cover goal setting, we'll suggest that the goals be very clear, achievable, and real. You must not let the ongoing situations or lower priority goals detract from your focus on your highest priority goal. If you're inconsistent, your Players will have trouble keeping focused.

Game Example: With a few seconds left in the conference championship football game, the Shadyside High School Oaks are down 7 points to the Kingston High School Monarchs. They're on the two yard line and there's time for only one play. The ball is handed to Freddy Foran, the Falcons' ferocious fullback, who breaks two tackles and drives into the end zone. Immediately, he is tackled and smothered by his teammates while Coach Cochran is going crazy on the sidelines: "Stop it! We're going for two! Get ready in there!"

The Learner at Play

The celebration continues long enough for Referee Richards to throw his flag and signal "Delay of game" and step off a 5 yard penalty.

What happened? It's Coach Cochran's problem. Throughout the season, he's allowed all kinds of celebrations after good runs, great tackles, and touchdowns. Every time that this happens the team loses its focus for the next play and concerns with the overall game situation have been set aside in order to have those rituals. Now, he has to settle everyone down and make them refocus on getting some kind of score. His need for a 2 point play has been jeopardized. Will he learn from this experience? Does he even realize what happened?

Tennis players will tell you that the best time to break your opponent's serve is right after she has broken your serve. Successes cause us to celebrate, which causes us to lose focus on our next task. We can minimize these distractions by keeping in touch with our higher priority goals – breaking serve is great – winning the match is better.

Instant Replay – With Focus: As Freddy breaks into the end zone, he tosses the ball to the linesman and goes back to get into the huddle with the other players. QB Ferguson is giving out orders, "O.K. guys, you know what we've got to do to win this one." He looks at Coach Cochran on the sideline, gets the signal to go for 2, and a sub is running in carrying the play call. "O. K., guys. Let's have Freddy do it again. Same play on one."

Freddy does it again – the players mob him and now it's time to celebrate.

The Learner at Play

Keeping Mentally Focused

Quarterback Ferguson and all of the players were in touch with and focused on the goal – to win the game. In order to do that, they had to go for 2 points. Other goals, including congratulations and celebrations, had to be put aside until the proper time.

The more excited we get about our successes, the more distressed we get over our losses. As I watch some coaches work, especially Joe Paterno, I see them having their players keep a steady emotional level. A pat on the back – "Nice going" – back to work focused on what needs to be done next. It's a very business-like operation – the priorities are always in mind and being worked on. Focusing is very effective for two reasons:

The Learner at Play

1. It keeps you actively in the game – it keeps you in touch with your goals; your mind doesn't wander into other worlds.
2. It sharpens your performance – it gives you a better, more intense target.

We know all about #1 – Emily is out in right field. There are no runners on base and pitcher Mindy is mowing them down with her fast ball – the opposing batters are not even getting foul tips. Emily really is looking forward to the pizza party she's been invited to this evening. Of course, just at that time, the right handed batter swings late and hits a fly ball – you know where. Emily wakes up just in time to misplay the easy out and the ball bounces off her glove – Error-9 – and a few hot team mates yell "Emily! Wake up out there." Emily wasn't focused. What do we do about that? Besides holler at her, that is.

All of us have experienced what Emily did – we have been caught back on our heels on defense or 'looking' with the bat on our shoulder in the batter's box unable to "pull the trigger." I suspect that this is part of the putting problem called the "yips" some golfers have.

Triggers

When we come to a complete stop and hold it for a time, we sometimes can't get into motion. Many golfers use a forward press to get things moving. Shooting free throws is similar – taking the ball from the official, going through a routine, and never coming to a prolonged dead stop. You will notice that the tennis player bounces the ball and keeps everything moving as he goes through the serving motion. And observe the player receiving the serve and how he moves his feet and racquet in order to be ready – so as not to be caught "flat footed."

One way to stay focused is to have a routine for every attempt. This routine must be gone through on every practice shot as

The Learner at Play

well as attempts during the game. For Sam shooting free throws, the routine may be:

Standing at the free throw line, he catches the toss from the official; he steps forward with one foot on each side of the center; he takes one bounce, he looks at the front of the rim; takes another bounce, he visualizes the ball taking a nice arc, going over the front of the rim, and into the net; he takes the ball up to eye level and makes a smooth stroke with a good follow-through. Next time he has a free throw he repeats the process, exactly. His routine has become 'automatic' and he maintains his focus.

Now, Herb may have a different routine. He may bounce the ball three times and twirl it in his hands before he looks at the rim. That's O. K., just so he keeps doing it that way.

Strategy #3 – Repetition

Correct practice creates a stable base and leads to improved performance.

The Falcons at Play

Coach Sara Garcia is out in center field helping Paula on catching flies and throwing directly to the plate. Bonnie noticed last game that Paula caught a fly ball flat footed and then threw too late to catch the runner on third who tagged up and scored. Bonnie has parent Geno Pacetti hitting nice, soft fly balls into short center field and she is demonstrating how to set up a couple of steps back and then move in to catch the ball and throw in one fluid motion. She is verbally describing what she's doing and she is asking Paula to verbalize what she's seeing.

Now Coach Garcia has Paula doing some dry runs, moving forward and pretending to catch the ball and throwing to the plate. After five attempts, Coach Garcia sees what she wants; a really good attempt; so she anchors it. "Looks good, Paula. Now let's take some real flies." Geno hits some more flies and Paula handles them all very well. Bonnie taps Paula on the left shoulder and says, "Good work. Now walk back to the fence and take a few minutes to visualize what you just did and get

The Learner at Play

into the good feelings – like that smile you had when you caught that last one and threw a one-hop strike to the plate."

Coach Garcia made sure that Paula handled the task well five times in a row. Then she gave her an anchor, a verbal reward on her most recent attempt, and the time and space to do a full visualization on sensory memory and positive feelings.

Comments

I remember teaching spelling to my fourth grade class and telling them to write each word 20 times (Did you hear the groans?). This operation is called 'Drill.' I soon noted that after about 5 good attempts the quality of the writing started going down and by the 15th attempt the words were either misspelled or illegible or both.

This meant that the last words they wrote, whose images were sent into their memory banks (Recency) were going to interfere with their ability to spell those words correctly. So, I got smart and my kids got happy – I told them to write each word five times and really focus on each one. They wrote very neat papers – their first and last attempts, (Primacy and Recency #1), were excellent models to store into their visual and kinesthetic memories. Their spelling improved as did their attitudes about spelling. I carried this over into my basketball coaching of skills.

The younger the player, the sooner she becomes bored with or just plain tired of repetitive actions.

Repetition and Focused Practice

When your kids are practicing they must be as focused as they are in the game. Practice does not make perfect – Practice makes Semi-Permanent.

Practice Session – Unfocused: Sam is at the foul line getting in the last few of his 25 shots and all he's doing is throwing the ball up there and Herb and Jason are rebounding his shots and "having fun" with the ball before getting it back to him.

The Learner at Play

This activity is not non-productive; it's counter-productive. Sam is actually practicing poor shooting and he will probably get very good at poor shooting – he is internalizing bad habits that will be present when the game situation is at hand.

Remember that practice doesn't make perfect – practice creates stability and if Sam isn't careful, bad foul shooting will become the stable condition. Every practice shot has to be made as if it's in a real competitive situation. Sam must go through all of the steps on each practice shot so that in the game his subconscious mind will take over and he will be operating in the performance mode.

When Does Fatigue Enter In With Your Kids

In terms of 25 shots, I think that's too many at one time. Sam, Herb, and Jason may not be able to concentrate on their task for that long a time. The younger the players are the fewer attempts it will take for them to lose concentration. They may make 10 good attempts and then slack off on their focus and begin making progressively poorer shots. One of the bad effects of this is that the latest attempts will be stored in the memory banks with more intensity than the earlier, better attempts. Fewer focused attempts are much better than more unfocused attempts. Have the kids shoot 10 free throws and rotate. I might even have them compete on how many they make on each 10 shot set.

Having the kids keep track of their percentage of successes each practice session and comparing that to their goals makes a lot of sense. However you do it, having your kids practice with a focused mind will make your practice more efficient and beneficial and will result in better game performance.

Other Sports

The need to practice skills by repetition is well represented in all sports; serving in tennis and volleyball, trapping in soccer, spiking in volleyball, running pass patterns in football, picking up the ten pin in bowling, putting in golf, etc.

The Learner at Play

Practice is different for different people. Some golfers, such as Vejay Singh, spend a lot of time at the practice tee while others seem to spend much less time practicing. It makes sense to have a standard, reasonable number of reps and then let those who want more to help themselves. Knowing when to stop practicing a skill is just as important as getting started.

Also, in cases where there is interaction between players, that interaction e.g., the quarterback taking the ball from the center, Practice, Practice, Practice.

"O.K. One more as good as the last one and we'll start on the forehand."

The Learner at Play

Strategy #4 – Anchoring

Storing your best performances so that you can bring them up when you want to improve your present performance.

The Falcons at Play

In the bottom of the sixth and the score is Colts 3 – Falcons 3. Doug was on 1st and Judy has just laid down a perfect sacrifice bunt down the 3rd base line. It was so good that the 3rd baseman had to let it roll hoping it would go foul. You now have runners on 1st and 2nd with no outs. The Colts' coach is out at the mound talking strategy with his infield.

It's the perfect time to anchor that bunt with Judy. First Base Coach Ames has just touched Judy on the top of her left shoulder and says, "Great job." (Tactile and Verbal Anchors)

Association

The basic idea behind anchoring is called association. We all have had experiences that we recall when we hear a certain sound, or smell a certain odor, or see a certain sight, or touch something. Whenever I walk into a bakery and smell freshly baked bread, I'm back in my kitchen at home waiting for my mother's bread to come out of the oven. We also have associations that we would like to forget and to avoid.

We want all of our players to associate good feelings with good performance. So, when Judy laid down that great bunt, Coach Ames made an association or anchor with a touch and positive comment. The entire process would have Judy include the whole experience in her memory banks. This is how the whole incident could have been recorded:

"Judy, how did that bunt feel?"

"Great, I had the bat in the right spot and loose enough so the ball didn't go too far." (Tactile)

"Right. What did you see?"

The Learner at Play

"Well, I only saw the first few feet but it was rolling real nice." (Visual)

"Right. How did the bat sound when it hit the ball?"

"Real good – nice ring." (Auditory)

"How do you feel about laying down that bunt?"

"Great – I got a hit out of it and I moved Doug up, too." (Feelings)

"You really ran it out well."

"Yeah, I didn't know he was going to let it roll so I took off as fast as I could run. (Kinesthetic)

That's it. All of the senses and feelings were experienced and anchored. The basic idea is for the player to get in touch with all of the good things that accompanied a successful experience and then to store them in such a way that they can be recalled for the next time that skill is to be used. The storing has to be as complete as possible, including all of your thoughts and feelings and all of the sensory factors; visual, auditory, kinesthetic, and tactile.

I learned and used this process from the Gestaltists – storing goals that have been attained so that you can retrieve the feelings and abilities when you want to use them again. A similar process is described by Raymond Floyd in his book, The Elements of Scoring. Floyd calls it "memory banking." While working with Dr. Don A. Blackerby, I became aware that Neuro-Linguistic Programming (NLP) has taken this technique much farther and made it much more effective and usable. I don't have the experience in NLP to give you their ideas so I will leave you to pursue that on your own if you wish. I highly recommend Don's book, Rediscover the Joy of Learning, for helping children in any area; sports, schools, or whatever. Dr. Blackerby would say, and did, that the process I described was overkill. Just let Judy enjoy the experience and fully record it in her memory banks. From the coach, a touch and/or "Nice job" would be enough.

A Revisit with a Self Anchor

Aaron is standing at the free throw line in practice. He throws up a shot that hits nothing but net. It had exactly the arc and rotation that Aaron wants. Aaron gets in touch with all of the actions and feelings of what he did – he then anchors the entire experience by rubbing the fingernail on his right forefinger with the pad of his right thumb. That's how he anchors his memory bank. (Bernice anchors hers with her secret word, "Bingo.")

It's game time: Aaron is standing at the free throw line with 2 free shots coming. His team is one point down and there's almost no time left in the game. Pressure, noise, pressure, waving banners, pressure, and general chaos prevail. Aaron does some deep breathing, closes his eyes for a moment, rubs the fingernail on his right forefinger with the pad of his right thumb, accepts the ball from the official, and goes into his free throw shooting routine. He has recalled his successful attempts and is asking his neurological system to perform correctly without stress.

Coaches' Anchoring

In the beginning of this chapter, Coach Ames gave Judy a tactile and a verbal anchor. In practice and in the game, Coach Ames watches for good performances and when he sees one, he gives the player an anchor touch.

He has given Judy many such anchors on offense and defense and now, as Judy is going up to bat, Coach Ames touches her on the shoulder and says, "Swing away and get that ball out of the infield."

Will This Work?

As in all cases, good psychology doesn't overcome poor performance skills. If your players are working on their skills, anchoring is a way for the coach to help them be more consistent. This works best when the kids learn to do their own anchoring and recall.

A Process for You

When I conduct seminars on Self-Motivation and Goal Setting, I begin by telling the participants to relax, close their eyes, and do some deep breathing. I would then instruct them to search their memory banks and find a time when they felt strong, potent, and productive. Then they were instructed to get deeply into that stored experience, to relive the feelings and thoughts that were there at that time.

Then I instruct them to anchor those feelings and thoughts and to bring them back into the seminar with them. This is having them recall situations that they have treasured and stored away in that special place we put them in. I would then have an audience of people who were more able to deal with the ideas and concepts being presented.

Lauren, one of my granddaughters, asked me to give her some advice on doing her best on the ACT test and I gave her some of the usual advice about keeping time, skipping tough questions and going on and coming back later (not getting stuck) to deal with them, and so on. Then I said, "Just before you begin the test, relax, close your eyes, and do some deep breathing. Search your memory banks and find a time when you felt strong, potent, and productive. Recall that time as vividly and completely as you can and then take those feelings and thoughts with you as you take the test."

Whenever I make a speech or do a presentation, I get to the room early and go through the same process. It's a lot better than that old advice about imagining that everyone in the audience is wearing pajamas (or whatever similar technique you may use).

Other Sports

The use of this process is the same in all sports and in all areas of learning. You all have had experiences that you have lovingly stored away – just keep storing them and bringing them up when you need them to help you in whatever you're doing.

The Learner at Play
Having Time for Anchoring

Kids need time and a structure for anchoring good performances after a game. I like to have a session after the game focusing on two areas;

1) What we did well in the game and

2) What we need to work on in our next practice.

Post Briefing Session Interview: Coach Barnes has just finished his after-game session with the hockey Bisons and the players are headed home. Let's talk to one of them. Hi, what's your name and can you tell us something about your coach and that meeting you just had with him?

"Hi, my name is Tony and I think my coach is the greatest. I really like our after-game meetings. Coach calls them his debriefing sessions, whatever that means. Anyway, we sit down and he goes over the things that we didn't do so good and he says to 'let go of them' and not to take them home with us – that we'll work on them next practice. And then he tells us to remember the things that we did right and to hang on to them. He gives us a little time to think about them – he calls it 'anchoring.'

"I like how he tells us what we did right and what we did wrong; he's never, "How many times have I told you to look where you're passing the puck?" Instead, he says, "Remind me to have you work on your passing next practice." He doesn't beat you over the head with what you did wrong – he works on getting you to do it right.

"I guess the main idea here is that I always know what Coach is thinking about my game because he tells me. I like that. My coach last year used to yell at us a lot. He never told us how to do it better – he just told us that we were doing wrong stuff and sometimes he just yelled at us and we didn't even know what he was yelling about. I didn't like that.

"I made a few mistakes today and I know what they were and I'm going to work on correcting them before the next game. I did some good stuff, too, and I know I can keep doing them because I remember what I did and how I did it."

The Learner at Play

Strategy #5 – Acting As If...

Having your actions change your attitudes and beliefs about yourself.

The Falcons at Play

Benny jumps out of his dad's car and heads straight for Coach Sara Garcia. The words almost shoot out of his mouth, "I've been thinking a lot after the last game and I want to be a really good player. Will you help me?"

"Sure, but what brought this on?"

"I was watching a pre-game interview with my hero, Kevin Durant, and he said if you're not really committed to excellence, you'll never be as great as you could be. Is that true?"

"Yes, that works in everything; playing a piano, learning math facts, whatever.

Why?"

The Learner at Play

"Well, I've been thinking that I haven't worked as hard as I can and I've just been bragging when I do something good. I don't deal with the stuff that I don't do well."

To herself, Sara says, "Wow, he may be on his way to losing his nickname, Benny the Braggart." Aloud, "O.K., let's set a goal that fits. 'I will be an All-Star' and an affirmation, "I am getting better and better all the time in all parts of the game.'
""Sounds good. Now what do I do?

"Do you have any idea how a great player acts in practice and in the game?"

"Sure, I watch Kevin Durant a lot. He's got real class."

"All right, from this minute on, whenever you're at practice or in the game you are going to act the way Kevin Durant acts in combination with how Benny operates." "Gotcha, I'm starting right now."

Models are great for this action. Just be sure to get good models in terms of good character and in your ability to see yourself doing what they do.

And Now For the Team

The Falcons have worked hard and have made it to the quarter finals of the city tournament. They're really nervous on the bench and Coach Doakes goes to work settling them down.

O.K., everybody sit down. We are going out on the field and take our warm-ups. I want you to look great and act great. Straighten up your suits. Pull up your socks, Get that cap on straight – we look like champions. When you get out on the field act the way the Red Birds did when we went to the city to watch them play – we act like champs. When you're playing, you'll always be doing your best because win or lose – we are champions."

Now, the Falcons are on the field and they are going through their drills with a lot of energy and pep talk and looking like champions. "If you want to be more outgoing, act as if you are outgoing." This also seems to be effective when a person hears the message from a significant other person – a child from her parent or teacher; a worker hearing it from his supervisor or a player hearing it from his coach.

An American Genius

When I became acquainted with the teachings of William James I added his process. James, the great American philosopher and psychologist, had a terrific idea for us teacher/coaches to use. In its simplest form, it may be called "Acting as if. . ." or "Going from Actions to Change." These ideas when put into appropriate action are very simple, straightforward, and effective. First, you have to identify something you don't have that you would like to have. For example, Jon, a teenager, has a problem with meeting people in a group such as in a party. He likes to think about it as "I'm shy." This has gotten him through life up to the present time, and now he would like to get to know new people (especially girls) and his problem is a problem.

Jon says to himself, "I need to learn how to talk to people." (Recognizing a need) "I'm going to talk to people from now on." (Setting a goal and being committed to it) "I'm going to attend that party for my school debate team." (Action) "I like the way Jody operates. She just kind of meanders around talking to people she knows and then moves over to strangers. I can see myself doing that." (Finding a model and visualizing)

So Jon goes to the party. He acts as if he is outgoing and he likes the result. He keeps it up by going to more parties and "Acting as if. . ." until one day he realizes that he is outgoing and he isn't acting any more.

This combines Self-Talk with Positive Expectancy to make the change in a person's behavior. Jon could not have set the goal, visualized the behavior, and acted on the change; if he hadn't been able to change. When he had made the decision to act, his subconscious mind would have told him he couldn't do it and no mental image would have come up. Also, if Jon believed that Jody and other socially adept kids had some talent that he didn't have that allowed them to be successful, he would never have made that big step. He would have said sub-consciously and even perhaps consciously, "I just can't be that way" and he would have talked himself out of trying and succeeding – that is Negative Self-talk.

The Learner at Play

I don't know where I got this story but I really like it and the point it makes...

Cutting Down The Nets – A Study in acting as if. . .

Stan Jones had had great winning seasons as the basketball coach of the small, rural high school in Underwood. He then moved up to a stronger conference and surpassed those records in small town Midway High School. He felt that it was time to move on to greater challenges so he accepted the head coaching position at suburban Brandon High School.

All the local citizens; school personnel, townspeople, and students; were friendly and cooperative and seemed to be genuinely happy to have a coach with his record come to their school. However, there was this disquieting message that was repeated over and over by almost everyone Stan met. In fact, he seemed to hear it a lot from students and players, "It's good to have you here, Coach, but Brandon has never had a winning team." What they didn't say out loud was, "And we don't think that we will ever have a winning team."

What an attitude to be confronted with and coming at him from all angles. What to do? At the beginning of the first practice, Stan had his players, the Brandon Bears, sit on the floor at one of the free throw circles. As he began talking to his players about his plans for the team this season, his manager brought out a ladder and set it up next to the nearby basket. Stan took a pair of taping scissors out of his pocket and handed it to Reese, captain of the team. "Fellows, it has been my experience that many teams upon winning tournaments do a poor job of cutting down the nets. Since we don't want our team to be embarrassed at those happy times, we are going to practice cutting them down correctly and with the right amount of enthusiasm.

Reese, you get up there and make the first cut. The rest of you guys give him the loudest support you can generate then take your turn cutting. O.K. team, let's do it!"

The Learner at Play

Practice as if you're champions and you'll play like champions.

Strategy #6 – Reinforcement/Feedback

Using the basic reward system to maintain your progress.

The Falcons at Play

At the crack of the bat, Coach Doakes groans. A sharply hit liner flashes through the hole between first and second. "Oh, no, that'll bring in two runs." Not yet – Paula charges in from short right field, picks up the ball on first bounce, and throws a strike to Connie, who has come over from the pitcher's box to cover first. "You're out!" calls Ump Jake Abrams. "That's 3 outs – let's go, in and out."

The first one to reach Paula as she comes in off the field is Coach Doakes, with high fives and "Great play! Fantastic throw!" She then grabs Connie, "Heads up play! That's the way to play the game!"

Comments

The Learner at Play

Immediate Reinforcement – The sooner you tie the reinforcement to the incident, the stronger it is. Coach Doakes did it right. However, there is another good way to do it. After Paula and Connie get the good stuff from their teammates, Coach Garcia, who has been working with the outfielders, sits down next to Paula and says, "You just made all the hard work you did in practice pay off. That was a terrific play – you are getting to be a terrific asset to our team." Coach Garcia did three things and did them well. First, she gave Paula a verbal reward for her actions just as the other coaches and players had. Second, this reward would have been less intense than the others because of the time lapse between the incident and the response, but she made up for that by giving her comments more intensity and tying it to her work in practice. Third, in addition to reinforcing what she did, she reinforced Paula for who she is as a person.

The reinforcement model is very simple to use – in fact, we all use it all the time. We use it with our children, our pets, our employees, our friends. We most often don't realize that we're using it. We also most often use it honestly and responsibly (but it can be used dishonestly and irresponsibly).

Often we reinforce people for what they do but we forget to reinforce and appreciate them for who they are.

Watch the "Dog Whisperer" – He has A Message for Coaches, too.

You want your dog to sit up; you say "sit", you sit him up; you say "good dog", you give him a dog snack. Next time when you say "sit" the dog sits and you give him another verbal reward and snack. If he doesn't sit, you very patiently go over it again. You didn't yell, "You stupid dog, what's wrong with you? Can't you learn anything?"

Are your players as worthy as Spot? My friend, Counselor & Coach Bill Farnham, told me, "If we treated our friends as we treat our players, we wouldn't have any friends left."

Negative Usage of Reinforcement

There is an old story that may be true about a prospector in the Old West who struck a mother lode. He was headed back East with his young son and several bags full of gold nuggets. He wanted his son to remember where the gold mine was so he stopped his wagon at several landmarks. He told his son to look at those landmarks and then spanked the dickens out of him so he would never forget them.

Of course, that's not what happened. Instead, his son stored all that information way back in his data banks with all of the other bad experiences that he wanted to forget. He never did get back to that mine.

What happens to your pitcher when all you do is holler at him for not backing up the catcher on a throw to the plate from the left fielder? What is he going to learn from his mistake?

A Mistake is a signal from the Learner to the Teacher that this is a place where he can be taught something he needs to know.

Lessons from the Animal Kingdom

There are some interesting examples of how animals can be conditioned so that we can establish their limitations.

When circus elephants are very young, they are tied to big, long stakes with big, heavy chains. As much as they try to get loose, they can't and soon they stop trying. The circus folks can then tie them down with small stakes and light chains. So you will see adult elephants tied down with light chains and wonder why they don't just pull away.

You can try this one. Put some fleas in a container, such as a glass aquarium, and you'll note that they can hop up and hop out. After chasing them down, cover the aquarium with a piece of glass. They will keep hopping for a while until they experience the futility of their efforts. Then you can take the cover off and not worry about their leaving.

In another instance, investigators put some mackerel and goldfish in the same tank. Ordinarily, the goldfish

The Learner at Play

would disappear into the mackerel but the people in charge being aware of this put a glass barrier between the two species. The mackerel kept trying to get to the goldfish and kept bumping their snouts so they finally gave up. The barrier was then removed and the goldfish swam among their large relatives without becoming dinner.

After The Game – The Debriefing Process

The Reinforcement Stage – Go over the things that went well. Be personal, use the active voice – "Terry, I like the way you handled the pitchers today. You're getting the idea that a catcher does more than catch the ball and throw out runners. Lester, you were really alert when you covered first on that bunt." etc., etc.

The Planning Stage – List the things that need to be worked on. State them positively and with affirmation. "Next practice is Saturday. We'll work on backing up throws from the outfield" and "We'll be improving our run downs."

A Follow-Up on the Elephant Story – It is also reported that if an adult elephant is scared enough, perhaps by a fire, he will break loose from his chains and the trainers will not be able to control him with chains again – he is called a Rogue Elephant.

Is this a metaphor for us?

Strategy #7 – Awareness

Knowing and using the whole picture.

The Falcons at Play

The liner ricocheted off Tim's glove at first base and bounced toward center field. Tim took off after it and ran it down. Terry, the catcher, had to stay at home because of the runner on second going to third and Bessie, the pitcher, was backing him up. Tim picked up the ball and saw that the batter had rounded first and come down the line but wasn't going to try to get to second. As Tim look toward first, there was Paula who had come in from right field to help out. The runner turned to go back just in time to see Paula waiting for the throw from Tim.

The Learner at Play

Good throw, quick tag, runner's out. All of the Reinforcement tactics are appropriate here.

Comments

How can you teach that? Paula saw the whole picture – she saw where she might be needed and she got there. Some people seem to have it and others never seem to get it. I attribute a lot of the problem to our teaching kids the game in a very narrow way. On the Herons basketball team, Curt is a guard and his coaches teach him all the guard stuff. He has no idea what the center does who has no idea what the guard does. Neither one of them knows what the forwards do, etc.

I have always felt that it was important for each of my basketball players to experience what each of his teammates was doing so during practices I had the guards play center for a while, the forwards played guard, the centers play forward, and so on. They soon not only knew what their teammates had to deal with, they also knew how to better interact with them, that is, better teamwork.

Isolated Practice and Context Practice

I think that we all spend too much time teaching skills and practicing with many repetitions separate from the real game conditions. This results in having the experience so far removed from the game situations that the practice may not be relevant. For example, the environment they're in when Sam and his teammates are practicing free throws is far removed from the environment of the real game. Also, the stress level and fatigue factors are different.

One answer is to do a lot of simulated practice with the whole team involved. Make the plays real. "O. K., guys, one out, runner on second." (And there is a real runner on second) A fly ball to right center. The second baseman goes out for a possible relay, the shortstop covers second, the third baseman covers third, the center fielder is catching the ball, and the right fielder is backing him up. That's it? Of course not. The pitcher is backing up the third baseman, the catcher is staying put, the first baseman waits at first until the catch is made and then he

The Learner at Play

heads for home to back up the catcher, the left fielder backs up third down the left field line – maybe the ball will be thrown to the catcher who then tries to get the runner who turned the corner and he makes a bad throw to third.

Ask this question a lot; what could you have done on that play that might have helped? In the example at the start of this section, Paula could have seen the play as very simple. The ball wasn't hit to her so there was nothing for her to do on this play. Just go back to her right field position and get ready for the next pitch – she knew better.

Coach Ames yelling, "That's the way to back up the 3rd baseman, Stan."

Bottom Line

Whatever your sport is, you have to teach your players all of the rules, all of the tactics, all of the operations of the game. Sometimes it's on the practice field, sometimes it's after the game, sometimes it's on the bench, sometimes it's on the playing field – but it's always there to do. I really enjoy watching the College Women's Softball World Series. If you want to see players really well drilled and knowledgeable about where to go and what to do on every play; watch those women play. It's a clinic.

Strategy #8 – Self-Talk and Affirmations

Using positive self-messages to achieve your goals.

The Falcons at Play

Larry has just come to the bench and says to his teammate, Tim, "I dropped that easy fly ball. I guess I really am a klutz." "Whoa," Tim hollers, "What did you just say about yourself?" "Oh, yeah, ERASE, ERASE. I'm getting to be a better fielder all the time."

> *Argue for your limitations*
> *And sure enough they're yours.*
>
> *Richard Bach – Illusions*

Self-Talk

The subconscious mind believes everything we say about ourselves and makes no judgment about whether it's something good or something bad. When we say something positive about ourselves, our subconscious mind says, "This is who and what I am and I will store it in that special place we call self-identity." When we say something negative about ourselves, our subconscious minds says, "This is who and what I am and I will store it in that special place we call self-identity."

Self-talk is the most important of the programming activities. You are aware of that 'inner voice' that speaks to you regularly, telling you about yourself and helping make the decisions that affect your actions and feelings. Many of these messages are 'negative' in nature. 'Negative' meaning that they prevent you from doing what you are capable of doing. 'Positive', on the other hand, means that the message is allowing or enabling you to realize your potential.

The Learner at Play
Your Players Will Talk – Listen To Them

Don't allow your players to say negative things about themselves. For example, "But, Coach, I've never been able to handle high pop-ups." As long as she affirms that, she will never be able to handle those high pop-ups. I usually say "Erase, erase." when I hear something like that and my players have gotten the message. They have learned to monitor their own self-talk, to catch themselves, and to put in the erase message. Affirmations are powerful statements about who we are and what we expect to become. These messages that we send to our psycho-cybernetic brain are instrumental in our choosing who we are, creating ourselves. We process millions of thoughts each day. We ask that marvelous brain that we have been endowed with to evaluate and act upon these self-selected messages.

The messages we carry in our minds run our lives. It is necessary to our growth and well-being that we put the correct messages into our minds

Talking Ourselves Out Of Achieving Our Goals

The following incidents have happened in my presence and I'll bet you have had similar experiences:

We are at the Pla-Mor Lanes. Andy is standing at the ball rack. He turns to us and says, "If I pick up this ten pin and get an 8 pin count I'll make 200. I've never bowled a 200 game."

Do you think Andy will pick up that spare and get an 8 pin count or better?

We are on the 15th hole on the Old Wayne Golf Course. Mike, a stranger, joined us at the first tee. He is playing decent golf and seems to be a nice guy. We are now on the 15th tee. Listen, Mike, is saying, "If I don't make another double bogie on the next four holes, I'll break 100. I've never broken 100." **Do you think Mike will play the next four holes in 4 over par or better?**

Our thoughts and statements become self-fulfilling prophecies and we tend to live them out.

The Learner at Play

Watch Your Language!!

The word, 'but' appears in many of the negative self-talk statements. "I would like to _____, but _____." One of my self-monitoring systems is being aware of how I use the word. 'But.' 'But' is often used as a stop sign and an invitation to make all kinds of statements that would keep us from achieving our wish. "I would like to learn to play bridge, but I have no card sense." Whenever I make a statement like that, I check what came after the 'but' and determine if it's the truth, if it's an excuse not to do it, or if it's an old, inaccurate message.

For example, Rick says to me, "I'll never be able to serve well. I'd like to, but I just don't have the arm speed." Is the part of that statement, ". . .? I just don't have the arm speed." true or false? Is it an excuse or is it a reason? Or is it a message that has been given to Rick so many times that he simply accepts it as truth. We don't know and we're not going to accept his statement until we've checked it out. We are going to set up an informal program for him to set a goal on serving better and harder, to learn some serving skills, and to write and say positive affirmations to override his negative affirmations.

On the other hand, 'and' is a go sign so Rick says, "I would like to be able to serve better, and _____." This invites Rick to make a list of the activities that will help him reach that goal, e.g., "I will double the amount of time I have been practicing my serving."

What Was That "Erase – Erase" Business?

We have a pretty good idea that thoughts and feelings are stored in short term memory banks for a while before they are cemented into the long term memory banks. Let's say that I say this about myself, "I'd like to do some writing, but I'm too lazy." (Erase – Erase) I want to be really clear about this – even if I wrote that sentence as an illustration for this book, the message was sent to my brain. I don't want it to stay there so I told my brain to erase it before it got saved into the hard drive.

The Learner at Play

I was giving a speech to a service club a few years ago and a member picked me up to take me to the meeting place. He kept making self-deprecating comments about himself and laughing, for example, "I was going to go to college but I didn't want to wear out my brain (Ha, ha, ha)." After several of these, I said, "Why do you talk so negatively about yourself?" and he replied, "Oh, I'm just kidding." Well, that brain of his didn't know that – it accepts what he said as the truth. The Subconscious Mind believes everything you tell it about yourself and everything you accept from others about yourself. We use three processes for identifying who we are. If we aren't alert and careful they will create a person we don't want to be. They can create barriers to our performance and can define limitations to who we are and what we can do.

The first process is Self-Talk – Self-talk consists of messages that we give ourselves that describe who we are, what we do, and how we do it and we often use it. Here are a few examples of Negative Self Talk:

- I've never been good in Math.
- I'm just a teacher (or whatever).
- I could be a winning coach, but I never get the good players.

The second process is agreeing with others when they describe who you are and what you do. This is especially strong if it is spoken by an adult who plays a significant role in one's life. If you allow other people to set limitations for you, they will become yours.

- My coach says I'm too clumsy and he must be right.
- My teacher told me that I can't write poetry so I'll have to do something else. Our family has never been lucky – lucky people get all the breaks

The third process has to do with "wisdom" sayings that have been repeated so many times that we think they are true:

- Big boys don't cry – they don't show their emotions.
- You can't teach an old dog new tricks.
- Girls aren't supposed to compete – it's not ladylike.

The Learner at Play

"Women can be musicians but they have to stay in their place."

My wife, Bobbie, has been a musician in two symphony orchestras. She wasn't breaking ground because there were other woman members before her – except that they were generally restricted to strings, harps, and flutes. Bobbie played the French horn and was one of the first women to break into the brass section. She heard a lot of negative comments but she had her goals and wasn't about to be stopped from reaching them. Did she compete with men? You bet and she won that first chair position, too.

I think that Title IX has been one of the greatest things that has happened in our history. Now, we can see the talent, desire, and self-motivation of women in softball, volleyball, soccer, and every other sports venue.

The Change Process – Self Talk

Monitor your players and have them change what they say about themselves.

Have them 'erase' what they said and replace it with a positive affirmation.

Personal messages:

From: "I can't field grounders hit to my right" (Erase, Erase)

To: "I'm a good all-around shortstop"

From: "I have trouble with knee-high, inside pitches" (Erase, Erase)

To: "My all-around hitting is getting better every day"

Team message:

Coach Pride's team is an enjoyable place to be. I am learning and improving in all ways every day. Everyone on this team has respect for every other person on the team. We care about ourselves and about each other. **For The Coach: Two Good Rules for Using Messages**

For herself: The Coach will talk about herself only in positive terms.

The Learner at Play

With the Players: The Coach will talk to her players and about them only in positive terms.

Affirmations

Affirmations are positive statements on what you intend to do – much more on this in Chapter 4.

"Look out where you want the ball to go – then hit it."

A Simple Goal Adjustment

My friend, Chris Smith, came to see me one day for some advice. He was co-managing a Tee Ball team. His son was

The Learner at Play

one of the players. It seems that his team was doing a poor job at the bat – they were hitting easy grounders in the infield.

I have observed that kids will hit down on the ball sitting on the tee. After all, they have the bat at shoulder level and the ball is lower. They are also looking down at the ball and hitting it where they see it; above the back center of the ball.

I suggested that he give the kids the advice in the caption. Look out to where you want the ball to go. Then swing to send the ball out there. You will see them drop down and level the bat before they swing. The following week, we went to watch a game. Chris was happy with the results. His kids were now hitting the ball to the outfield.

Strategy #9 – Visualization

Using your "mind's eye" to speed up your progress.

The Falcons at Play

It's the top of the seventh and the Falcons are one run down to the Owls. They have a runner on second and there's one out. Doug Meddors, the Falcons' best long ball hitter is at the plate. Coach Appel of the Owls is at the mound talking to his ace pitcher. "Harry, Doug likes high fast balls. We'd like to get him out but if he walks we'll have a chance for a double play. So be careful and whatever you do, don't give him a high fast ball."

Question #1–What's wrong with Coach Appel's directions to Harry?

Coach Appel no sooner gets back to the dugout than Harry lays a high fast ball on Doug and Doug loses it over the left field fence. "I told you not to give him a high fast ball," he yells. Harry is standing there wondering what happened. He didn't mean to get that pitch up in the strike zone – it was supposed to be down, knee high. Harry settles down and gets the next two batters out. He comes back to the dugout shaking his head and trying not to get mad at Coach Appel who is chewing him out.

Well, Harry is the first batter for the Owls in the bottom of the ninth. Bessie Anders is pitching for the Falcons. She tries to get ahead in the count but her curve ball hangs and Harry hits

The Learner at Play

it to the fence in left center and goes into second standing up. Coach Appel is talking to Dale Waters, the next batter. "We want to move him up to third so we can bring him home with a fly ball or squeeze. Lay a bunt down the third base side but make sure you don't hit it too hard or directly at the 3rd baseman."

Question #2 – What's wrong with Coach Appel's directions to Dale?

Coach Appel gets back to his third base coaching position in time to watch Dale lay down a bunt directly to Connie at third who turns and catches Harry coming up the line. Harry tries to get back but gets caught in a rundown back toward second and tagged out. Dale has to stop at first. Coach Appel is steaming and Dale is standing on first base looking everywhere except in the direction of the third base coach. He's listening to Assistant Coach Billy Welch who is saying, "O. K., there's only one out. We're still in the game. We can't take too many chances – you're the tying run now. If the ball is hit in the infield, try to mess up any double play attempt."

Meanwhile, Coach Doakes of the Falcons is out at the mound. She has called all the infielders and the catcher in. "O.K., let's settle down. The tying run is still on base. Stay focused – our goal is to get this batter out even if the runner advances. Go for a double play if the ball is hit sharply; otherwise take a sure out either at second or first. Now, Connie, it's very important to keep the ball in the infield if he hits it so keep throwing your curve. Just snap it off a little more so it breaks better and keep it low and outside to this lefthander. What did I say, Connie?" "Snap off the curve and keep it low and outside."

Question #3 – What's right about Coach Doakes' directions to Connie?

Jack Henderson, the lefty, is ready to hit and he goes after the first pitch; low and outside just as Coach Doakes told Connie to pitch. The ball is hit sharply to Stan Simmons at short, who goes to his left, comes up with the ball, flips it to Lester at second base who evades Dale's frantic slide and relays it to Tim at first for the DP. The game's over.

All right, all together now – let's all visualize not going to the game tonight.

You Can't Visualize Something That Doesn't Exist

Well, then what do we visualize? Harry's right brain tried to form a visual of what the coach said to do but his mind couldn't make a visual of what not to do, so it made a visual of what to do. It formed a visualization of "let up on him", "high ball", and "above the waist." Also, Coach gave him a double negative message: Don't do something wrong – instead of a positive message: Do something right.

Visualization is a right brain activity. It's also called Mental Imagery. It's our ability to "see" something in our "mind's eye." We can create ourselves doing things the way we want them to be done. We can see ourselves making free throws (nothing but net), hitting drives down the middle of the fairway, breaking a curve ball knee high on the inside corner.

It also gives direction to our actions. For example, if I'm hitting my drive on the 8th hole over a pond and I focus on the water, I am more apt to hit the ball into the water. Especially, if I say to my partners or to myself, "I always have trouble getting over this water hazard."

The Subconscious Mind cannot distinguish between a real experience and a richly developed visualization. In his book, Tin Cup Dreams, author Michael D'Antonio tells about professional golfer Tom Kroll's caddy who warned him that there was out-of-bounds on the right. Kroll snapped, "Don't tell me those things. I don't need to be reminded of trouble." Kroll was probably visualizing hitting his drive long and down the middle. He didn't need another visual interfering with it; especially that kind of visual.

There's internal and external visualization. With the internal type, I would look down the fairway and see the ball flying from the tee and taking the desired path. Externally, I would watch myself at the tee box as I swung my driver and went through the activity.

The Learner at Play

Your mind is a rich creator of images – Here's a gimmick I use in my clinics: "Okay, relax now and do exactly what I tell you. For the next ten seconds, don't think of a pink elephant with green polka dots." What is your mind doing right now?

You Can't Visualize Something That You Can't Do

That marvelous brain of ours sure keeps us honest. My putting in golf has always been quite good and I can still visualize dropping long puts. However, the story with my drives is quite different. I used to be pretty long off the tees but now I'm about 30 to 40 yards shorter.

I could hit it over the trees on the dogleg right 4th hole back home so I would be able to visualize doing it and did it. Now, when I stand on that tee, my mind will not allow me to create that picture. So, I look down the fairway and see that I can hit it to the bend in the dogleg and that's what I do.

We can visualize only what we are capable of doing.

Another Coach; another Messed Up Message

A couple of years ago, Bobbie and I were watching a championship figure skating event. We were rooting for our favorite skater and we listened as her coach was giving her his final directions. Something of this sort, "Be careful on that double Axel – you have been over rotating it lately. And you have been going into that last jump too fast and not getting enough height." This was the last thing she heard before she skated to the center of the rink. Figure skaters do a lot of visualizing and the last advice she got from her coach gave her two very bad visual images.

Bobbie and I looked at each other and said simultaneously, "Oh, no!" We don't know if that advice caused a problem but sadly, what we were concerned would happen, did happen. Our skating favorite made some critical errors and didn't get the gold medal.

Visualizing Is More Than Visual – Let's Anchor It

It may sound like a contradiction but when we use visualization, we use more than visual. In Section #5 we dealt with Anchoring. After I hit that nice high drive with just a shade of fade into the middle of the 4th fairway I can anchor and store the sight of it, the crisp sound of the club head hitting the ball, the nice solid feel of the club in my hand, and all of the kinesthetic movements of my body. What if I hit a bad drive? I don't anchor it.

"Pick them up at mid court"

At a clinic in which we were presenting programs, Bobby Simpson told this story about one of his coaching instructions and the results. He was coaching a sixth grade basketball team and he wanted to change to a tight man-to-man defense, so he said to his players, "Pick up your man when he crosses the center line." I'll bet you know what happened. Well, put yourself in their shoes – what would you have done?

Teaching Visualization to the Kids

The process is simple so keep it simple. The simplest action to use in basketball is free throw shooting. First, model it with your kids so they can see you doing it. Stand at the free throw line with them sitting on the floor to the side and facing you. They'll know what you're talking about. Use the appropriate actions with your words.

"I'm looking at the back of the rim and I'm watching the ball leave my hand and take a nice arch and go through the hoop – nothing but net." Close your eyes and go through the motion without the ball.

Research and Visualization

The first research was done at the University of Chicago in the 1930s. The work was done in a physical education with free throw shooting. A large class was separated into three groups. In each group, the students took a lot of free throws and a record was made of each of their performances. The first group continued to attend class and practiced free throw shooting every day. The second group was told that they didn't need to attend class and to return at the end of the course period. The third group was given instruction in storing their successful attempts and in visualizing them – after a while they stopped the shooting and just visualized. At the end of the course, the first group improved 24%, the second group showed no change in performance, and the third group improved 23%. We don't know what would have happen if good practice and visualization were combined.

A long continued line of research has been done in this area. In 1974, B. R. Bugelski found that most investigations show that subjects who do physical practice followed by mental practice usually do just as well as subjects who do all physical practice, and that subjects who are visual imagers do better than those who are low in imagery.

This kind of research has continued formally and informally since that time. Informally, you will find a lot of good articles in sports magazines. Formally, many studies of the same design have been conducted for all kinds of physical skills (high jumping, piano playing, dart throwing, gymnastics, and others), with generally similar results.

Primary teachers should be careful about saying, "Don't run in the halls" to their kids. What image are they giving them?

Models – Your Idols and Your Own

Your players have several models that they can copy. Their parents were probably their first coaches and models. They have watched games live and on television and have stored visual images of many players, especially the play of their idols. For example, Beth watched our Olympic women's soccer team and has a lot of those images stored. You can furnish them images of players by using tapes such as training tapes furnished by your sports association. You can video tape your players in action. Professional, college, and high school

The Learner at Play

coaches tape their practices and games. These tapes can be used in two ways:

- Point out the errors that Scott made in his pass blocking and discuss with him how to remedy them. Be careful not to anchor the image.
- Cut out and assemble a bunch of the excellent moves that Scott has made and let him watch himself.

Have Scott store them in his memory banks so that he can recall them and repeat them.

Strategy #10 – Achievement

Attaining your goals; the only real measure of success.

The Falcons at Play

We're at the End of the Season Award Banquet and in this picture we see Coach Hall of the Tigers handing the Sportsmanship Award trophy to Colby, a member of his team. Stan Simmons of our Falcons will be accepting the Most Valuable Player Award.

What is "Success?"

Here's an excerpt from an article I wrote several years ago for another publication:

The Learner at Play
Winners and Losers
How do we separate the Sheep from the Goats?

I was watching a report on the New York Marathon on the news last night. There were 14,000 starters, 2,465 of them women; who planned to run the 26+ miles.

The first person to reach the finish line was Alberto Salazar. Bill Rodgers, who was trying for a fifth first place finish, came in fifth. Grete Waitz was the first woman finisher. She placed 74th overall and set a new woman's record for the marathon run. Pattie Catalone was the first American woman to cross the finish line. She wanted to become the second woman (joining Waltz) to break the 2 hour, 30 minute mark. She came in at 2 hours, 29 minutes, and 34 seconds.

The stories in the television coverage focused on these four and a number of others who had finished; an elderly person, a heart attack survivor, an amputee, a wheel chair contestant, and some first-timers. With that information, here are some questions:

- Was Salazar the winner and the other 13,999 losers?
- Was Rodgers a failure for not reaching his goal?
- Were the heart attack survivor, the amputee, and the wheelchair contestant losers?
- Was Waltz a loser? Was she the winner of a special group?
- Was Catalone a winner because she set a new personal best time and reached her goal of breaking 2 hours, 30 minutes? She came in 80th overall.

Let's take this in a broader view. Who determines whether you are a winner or a loser? Can you decide if someone else is a winner or a loser? How much do we allow others to judge whether we are successful and how much judging of others do we do? And then the last biggest question, after you decide who the losers are; what do you do with them?

Winners in the Survival Game

Business leaders, the smart ones, know that "Survival of the Fittest" is not logical. There can be only one Chief Executive Officer and you can't kill off the rest of the organization. Everyone in the corporation must believe that he or she is a Winner; the comptroller, the sales manager, the plant manager, the foreman on the line, the die maker, the typist, the grounds keeper, everyone. If you make any of them losers, you diminish the whole operation.

> **Success is being where you are after you've done your very best.**

The T-shirt read, "Second Place is the First Loser"

When I saw that t-shirt, I wanted to tell the young man wearing it to take it off and burn it. What a negative message! I'm an avid golfer so if I don't win the club championship, I'm a loser? Not on your life! There are 32 teams in the National Football League. Sometime in January we have a Super Bowl Game and one of the 32 is crowned The Big Winner. Are all of the rest of the teams losers? I hope the 31 non-champion teams don't quit because they didn't win the championship.

Losing a game doesn't make you a 'loser.' What you do and who you are, are two different things. You can lose and not be a loser. You can be, act, and feel like a winner regardless of the circumstances. And when you do your very best, you are always a winner.

And so it is with your team. The players, the parents, your assistant coaches and you, must all feel that you are winners. Also, you might want to consider the effects of making some of your players winners and others losers. If any of your players feel inadequate, the whole team suffers.

Success; a Personal Viewpoint

Success is a personal creation; it just doesn't happen by accident. Of the many definitions of success I have found, this statement by Paul J. Meyer seems to me to be the most exact:

The Learner at Play

Success is the progressive realization of worthwhile, pre-determined personal goals.

Paul J. Meyers

Success is personal; it is the result of reaching your personal goal. It is goal oriented; if you aspire to be a realtor, being a bank teller is not being successful. For someone else with the goal to become a bank teller, becoming a bank teller is success. Your goals must be worthwhile to you; they must be aligned with your value system; the must be acceptable to your attitudes about yourself and your perception of the world around you.

Goal setting and reaching, therefore, are extremely important. To become a success in your own mind, you must set goals that are meaningful to you, that will, when reached, enable you to feel successful.

I am currently reading a biography of one of my favorite sports figures; Vince Lombardi. Was Vince Lombardi successful? I don't know. I don't know what his goals were. From our point of view, he was a great success as a football player and as a coach, but that is our perception. What were his dreams, his visions, and his life goals? Only he, and to some degree those who were close to him and loved him, knew his own personal marks of success.

I hope, that in all of his roles of player and coach, father and husband, religious person and all-around good human being; he believed that he had reached his goals and was a success.

Strategy #11 – Closure

Completing tasks so that you can move on to new ones.

It's time to finish this chapter so let's examine another concept that is very important in your interaction with the Kids even though it's really not a habit forming strategy. It's completing one task so that you can move on to next one.

The Falcons at Play

The Learner at Play

Coach Ames has just completed a field session on backing up throws with his group. The kids are sitting on the bench in the third base dugout. "O.K. Where does the pitcher go when there's a runner on second and the batter has hit a single into left field. Judy." "I would go behind the catcher and a little bit down the first base line." "Good, where does the catcher go if there's no one on base and the ball is hit to the shortstop? Tim." "He takes off down the first base line." "Good, where does the shortstop go with a runner on first trying to steal second? Doug." "If he has the bag he goes there to take the throw otherwise he goes behind the second baseman who is taking the throw." "Good, OK, that's it for now. Get ready for batting practice."

Comments

Coach Ames has closed one task so that he and the players can go on to the next task. Closure is also for the completing of things that are keeping you from moving on. When your mind is bugging you, it often means that you didn't complete something – complete it so that you can move on. When we complete the issue we can then get on with other issues.

This is the example I use in workshops about our everyday life issues:

You have been painting your living room in that soft blue color you really like and unfortunately you run out of paint with just about 2 square feet left in the corner. Being very resourceful, you move one of your end tables in front of it so no one can see your unfinished work.

But! You know it's there and every time you walk into your living room your little mental reminder program says, "I've got to finish that paint job one of these days." Finally, after about a dozen episodes you go down to the store and get a small can of the same paint and complete the job – Closure – and you can walk into that room without being bugged by your brain.

When your mind keeps bugging you, it often means that you didn't complete something – complete it so that you can move on.

Conflict Resolution

The Learner at Play

The entire concept of conflict resolution is based on closure. At the beginning of this chapter Coach Doakes was really concerned about how Clara the Clown used her antics when they were inappropriate. How can they come to some resolution? Instead of sitting on it and being bent out of shape, Coach Doakes operated in such a way that she got closure on an issue that had been bothering her. This closure enabled both her and Clara to move forward with their team goals.

It ain't over "til it's over" – **and then it's over.**

Let's Get Closure on This Chapter

Here are some wrap-up thoughts on this chapter. Then we can move on to the coaches' jobs in this whole process. So that you may help your players develop their potentials to their fullest, you can follow two key principles:

NEVER doubt your players' potentials.

NEVER think in terms of limits to their potential.

Sandy and the Outlet Pass

The fast break I learned in college and used as a junior/senior high coach is diagramed here. We want the guard on the side the ball is rebounded to clear out to that sideline. The rebounder passes the ball to him and he gets it to the opposite guard in the center of the court and takes off down his outside lane. Any member of the front line who's free takes the other outside lane. If we get a three-on-two we are going to score.

The Learner at Play

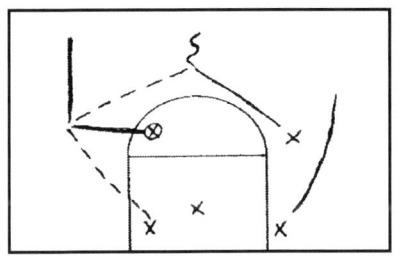

Strategy #1 – Primacy/Recency

Coach Haley introduces Sandy to the Outlet Pass by having him watch a drill the older players are running. At the end of the practice session, Coach Haley sits down with Sandy and outlines the play on his clipboard. Sandy goes home feeling pretty good about working the play.

Strategy #2 – Focus and Triggers

Coach Haley keeps Sandy focused during the practice session by reminding him of the goals of the fast break – to get the ball out quickly and then get it to the center of the floor. Every time the ball is shot toward the hoop, unless Sandy has a chance for the rebound, he heads for the outlet pass spot, ready to head to the center if the ball goes to the other side.

Strategy #3 – Repetition

Coach Haley has Sandy go through getting into position many times, watches for some good repetitions, and when he sees several of them in a row, he calls that part of the practice over.

Strategy #4 – Anchoring

Coach Haley sees that Sandy has it down pat now. Right after a really good effort, he says, "O.K., Sandy, go sit on the bleachers for a while and recall everything you did on that last play."

Strategy #5 – Acting as if...

Coach Haley, "I noticed in your journal that one of your favorite athletes is Roger Federer. This isn't tennis, but can you imagine how he would make this play? You can? O.K., go do it."

Strategy #6 – Reinforcement

The Learner at Play

Every time Sandy makes a good effort, Coach Haley says enthusiastically, "Great job, Sandy." When Sandy doesn't do well, the coach says in a calm voice, "Let's try it again." How many times does he do that? As many as it takes.

Strategy #7 – Awareness

Coach Haley, "When you go out to get the pass, what does the other guard do?" Sandy, "He takes the center lane and I get the ball to him." Coach Haley, "And the opposite forward or center?" Sandy, "He fills the opposite lane." Coach Haley, "And you?" Sandy, "I beat it down the floor in my lane."

Strategy #8 – Self-Talk/Affirmations

Coach Haley says, "Great practice session, Sandy. I see you have your journal with you. This would be a good time to write an affirmation." Sandy sits down and writes. "I'm always in the correct place so we can use the outlet pass to start the fast break."

Strategy #9 – Visualization

As he had learned to do with other skills, Sandy took a copy of the diagram home and that night when everything was quiet, he "saw" himself making the correct moves – and doing them perfectly every time.

Strategy #10 – Achievement

Coach Haley had given Sandy a copy of "My Goal Achievements" and he filled out his successful achievement while he was doing his visualizing.

Strategy #11 – Closure

"Coach, I've worked hard on the outlet pass and I've got it down pat." Coach Haley, "I agree, so let's move on to running the lanes." Coach Haley and Sandy have effected a closure on one skill and the space has opened up for them to move on to a new skill.

Chapter 3

The Coach - A Professional Teacher

The Coach — A Professional Teacher

> **The Coach/Leader's Toolbox**
> **Working With Your Kids**
>
> This section deals with the Toolbox, the skills, teaching techniques, and strategies that we Coaches need to know in order to have our Kids learn how to play the game better and to be able to use their skills more effectively.
>
> Often when I talk to coaches about sports psychology, they will say something of this sort, "'Yeah, I'd like to use more of that with my kids.'" The trap here is that you have to know the ideas of psychology and how to use them before you can use them on or with your kids.
>
> This section is for you to learn more than you already know about Motivation, Positive Expectancy, Readiness, and other skills tools so that you can use Anchoring, Focus, Affirmations, and those eight other strategies effectively with your kids.

The Coach – The Teacher

Now we'll be looking at how to implement all of the strategies that we presented in Chapter 2. This is the "Teacher's Edition" that we all wished we'd had when our fourth grade teacher told us to do all of those division problems on Page 34.

In a very real way, your practice and playing fields are classrooms. A good coach studies about how people learn and uses this information to teach new skills and reinforce already learned skills. She is an expert in motivating players. She knows about the power of positive reinforcement and she uses it to help her players become better people and more skillful players. You can be like that terrific coach/teacher and you can

The Coach — A Professional Teacher

teach your kids the skills of the game, the rules of the game, the strategies of the game, and above all, the joy of the game.

We are going to be dealing with the coach as a professional teacher, using all of the good stuff that we know works when the expert teacher deals with the student who wants to learn. Almost all of the kids who come out for sports really do want to learn. This is a big advantage over the classroom teaching situation. Motivation is simply not the problem on the field of play as it is in the classroom.

Most of the kids are interested in playing the game and playing it well. There's not a lot of resistance to instruction and even "homework." Yes, there are some kids who don't want to be there – they're there because someone else wants them to fulfill their goals (as in, "My kid is going to be a champ just like his Old Man.") It's up to us to help that kid get the most out of a situation that is not right for him or even get out of that situation.

As coaches, our task is simply the same, to take this eager bunch of kids and make them better at what they're doing.

There Are No *Tabula Rasas* Here

An old psychological concept was that kids are born with a tabula rasa, a blank slate of knowledge and thoughts. Although they may not have tabula rasas they have had many physical activity experiences. Kids not only want to be there playing the game but they already have had some experiences and a lot of interest. Our job is to help them by extending what they have already learned, fixing what they learned wrong, and helping them learn new ways of playing the game.

Positive Expectancy

Positive expectancy, the positive use of the Self-fulfilling Prophecy, is the necessary condition for a positive thinking model to work successfully. The Coach must have a firm and fervent belief that the process will succeed and be willing to go the extra mile to ensure its success. This is especially true when we're dealing with children.

The Coach — A Professional Teacher

The Falcons at Play

Lester had joined the team this year transferring from the Jaguars where he has been labeled a hard-headed kid, a trouble maker. During an off-season meeting, the Falcons' coaching staff had decided that in Lester's case, as in all cases, they would have a positive expectancy operation going with an additional checking on their progress. Coach Gene Ames, who deals more with the infielders, is to take Lester under his wing and make him feel that he's an important part of the team.

It is the first practice session and Gene has been helping Lester sharpen up on his footwork around first base. Lester had been a little leery about being transferred to a new team and some of his lack of self-confidence was showing up. Gene was doing a good job and felt pretty good about the session. He'd used a lot of affirming and verbal rewarding and had kept from getting into conflicts. When Lester said, "Why do I have to learn this stuff?" Gene replied, "Because it will make you a better player and isn't that what you want to be?"

(Remember that line; it's one of the best for communicating effectively with your kids.)

Lester was surprised. He expected the kind of answer that he got from Coach Harris of the Jaguars, "Because I said so – do it or get off the field." **Have you ever thought about the great opportunity you have when you get a kid from a team or take over a team whose coach isn't nearly as good as you are?**

Combined with Positive Expectancy is the Self-Fulfilling Prophecy. At the pre-season meeting, Falcon Coach heard Coach Harris say, "I'm sure glad to get rid of that Bingham kid. He drove me crazy with his questions and kept giving me that backtalk. He might have been an OK player but his attitude was terrible. I finally just gave up on him and told him and his Dad, who's just like him, that he would never be worth anything as a ball player." When Coach Doakes talked to Mr. Bingham she said, "I expect Lester to be a big help to our team this year. I watched him last year and thought he had great potential." Mr. Bingham told this to Lester and they both changed their way of talking about Lester's status using Coach Doakes' positive viewpoint.

There is Negative Expectancy with its self-fulfilling results. Go back to the coaches' meeting on Lester and replace what's there with, "Well, he's not going to get away with any monkey shines here." and "If he doesn't shape up, he's outa here."

The Illness Model

Many of the teams I watch are coached under what I call the Illness Model. The basic idea behind the Illness Model is that there is something wrong with the players and they need to be fixed. You will hear these coaches say. "The kids who come to me can't run, hit, throw, or anything and it's my job to teach them the basics." The communication from Coach Harris to his players is, "You can't do this so I have to show you how to do it." He is always dealing with his players in terms of their "defects."

The real danger to this is that some of the kids can begin to take the negative advice personally. After being told time and time again that what they do is not O.K. they can start to believe that who they are is not O.K. They can get into some really unhealthy thinking, "Coach Harris keeps telling me that I can't do anything right so there must be something wrong with me." Basically, the kids won't enjoy a healthy, safe experience in the environment built by Coach Harris.

The Illness Model is an example of Negative Mental Attitude, the misuse of the Self-Fulfilling Prophecy. In most cases and in its use with most people, it is also not an accurate description of reality.

And The Wellness Model

Coach Doakes has a different idea about kids and their abilities. She sees them as people in process – growing and learning. "All of the kids who come to play on my team are O. K. They already know how to run, hit, throw, and so on and they come to practice ready and willing to learn how to do those things better. My job is to help them improve themselves." In Coach Doakes' world, the children are in a safe, healthy learning environment and they have the feeling of being O.K. people.

The Wellness Model accepts children as they are; healthy, growing human beings who have come to learn the game from caring, intelligent adults who will help them to grow and to be successful. When we say we help them "improve their skills,'" we are telling them that they already have these skills to some degree. Our job is to help them learn how to do these skills better – to improve on what is already there. The attitude of Coaches Doakes, Ames, and Garcia is consistently heard, "O.K., Larry, let's see you shag some flies – good catch – use two hands – that's better – set your feet before you throw – good, let me show you – try it again – you're doing great, just keep working on it."

"I Don't Know How To. . ."

Let's watch Winnie the Whiner as she does her thing during batting practice. "But, Coach, I don't know how to bunt." Coach Ames, "Great, here's the bat.

Show me how you stand and hold the bat when you are going to bunt." Winnie gets into a decent stance and holds the bat in at least a semblance of a correct way. Coach Ames, "Good start – now pull your left foot back a little so you're facing the pitcher – Right! – Now slide your right hand down a little farther. Let's try one. . ." and he goes ahead with Winnie building on what she already knows and can do.

Start with them where they are and then take them to a better place.

Where they are is O.K. and the new place will be even better. We will be using this model throughout this book – helping players improve on the skills and game awareness they already have. My friend, Dr. Robert Grupe, went to a printer and asked him to print a book-cover a certain way. He said, "It can't be done that way." Robert said, "If it could be done, how would you do it?" The printer said, "Well, first I would . . ." and he went on to explain how it could be done.

Positive Expectancy and Self-fulfilling Prophecy

The literature of the world is full of the effects and power of the Self-fulfilling Prophecy and Positive Expectancy. People in leadership/parenting/teaching roles have expected good things to happen and they did. (There also is Negative Expectancy when we have expected bad things to happen and they did.) In schools, we talk about the Hawthorne effect. There are the true stories of teachers mistaking children's locker numbers for I.Q. scores and creating good results from "'slow learners'" and of principals misplacing good students with a remedial teacher and finding that previously 'well-behaved' children had become 'discipline problems'.

A Real Self-Fulfiller

Children have many expectations and it's the master teacher who helps them to realize their expectations. Several years ago, I was teaching at Elmhurst College with Dorothy Faegre. Dorothy was a professor in the Math Department but she had a great interest in the education of elementary school teachers so she and I had many occasions to share thoughts.

One day, during a discussion on positive attitudes and learning, she told me this story about the teacher her children had when they entered school in the first grade. This happened in the days before kindergarten and pre-school were on the scene. Other than I can't recall the teacher's real name, here is her story:

MOMMY, DADDY, I LEARNED HOW TO READ TODAY!

My children had a most marvelous teacher, Mrs. Bright. She taught in a rural school; grades 1-4. I was always amazed at the attitudes my children had about school. They came home all excited and happy. When I picked them up at school, I noticed that all of the other children had the same attitudes.

One day I had time to talk with Mrs. Bright and asked her how she managed to accomplish this. She said, "Children come to school expecting certain things to happen. For example, the first graders come to school expecting to learn how to read. They have been told by parents, older children, and other

The Coach — A Professional Teacher

adults that they will learn to read. To children this does not mean that they will learn to read sometime during the year; it means that they will learn to read when they go to school – the first day.

"'So the first day, we learn how to read. We make up a simple, little story about anything that is happening; the weather, a game, snack, our recess. I write the story on the board and we "read" it together. I make a copy for each child to take home and "read" to the parents."

Some of the simplest techniques that we use with people are the most powerful. The children had a goal, a need to be fulfilled, and Mrs. Bright helped them to reach their goal, to fulfill their need. The setting and reaching of personal goals is crucial and when we assist others in this process with the expectation that they succeed, we will elevate their self-esteem and their performance. And yes, we can take some credit in this achievement and take enjoyment in observing the growth.

Mommy, Daddy, I learned how to hit the backhand today!

The Coach — A Professional Teacher
Readiness

Your 10 year old son says, "Dad, I want to drive the car."
You say, "No."
Your 10 year old son says, "Why not?"
And you say, "Because ————."

Whatever reason you give, you are saying to him that he is not ready to take on that task. That's called "Readiness." Kids come to our great game in all stages of physical, mental, and emotional readiness. There are things they are ready to do and to learn and there are things they can't do and learn at that time. No matter how hard you may work with your 10 year old son, he is not going to be able to drive your car.

I was talking about this recently in one of my seminars and Jim told about this incident that happened in a Tee Ball game. This little fellow was on second when the ball was hit and he headed for third. And as little fellows do, he got to the base and stopped. The third base coach waved his arms and shouted, "Go home! Go home!" Well, that little guy broke down in tears and started running over to his parents in the stands. He had been told to go home by his big leader and he did so want to keep playing. This little person was ready for some things, but his baseball vocabulary and his conceptual knowledge of the game weren't up to dealing with that situation.

I see so much 'Over coaching' going on. Coaches standing in the third base coaching box giving elaborate signs, teaching youngsters intricate pick off plays, and demanding fancy pitches. The simple fact is that children are not at the stage of development that allows them to learn all those things that we have acquired over 20 or more years of playing. Each player is at his or her stage of development; they are where they are, not where we would like them to be or where they are supposed to be.

I like what Dr. James Hymes told us teachers of young children:

The Coach — A Professional Teacher

"Everybody is ready, it's up to you to find out what they are ready for."

The expert coach knows his skills, he knows his players and he matches them up. That little fellow playing Tee Ball was ready to do some things on the field but he had a little problem with knowing about "going home." I hope his coaches were understanding and caring people. You see, if they could not accept him as he is, they won't be able to help him grow and learn.

The Laws of Readiness

A long time ago, in Child Psych 401, I learned a lot about the concept of readiness and I was really impressed with the work of E. L. Thorndike. He had come up with some really practical ways of looking at readiness and what we teachers should do about it in working with our kids and I knew they would work in my classroom.

He stated his ideas in his three Laws of Readiness. He used basic behavioristic terms so I translated them to fit the actions I was performing with my 6th graders. When I was coaching, I simply made another translation so that I could use them on my basketball court or baseball field. Anyway, here is how they look on the court or field or arena or wherever:

- If Kristen is ready to learn how to hit the ball and she is allowed to hit the ball, she will have a happy experience.
- If Kristen is ready to learn how to hit the ball and she is not allowed to hit the ball, she will be frustrated.
- If Kristen isn't ready to learn how to hit the ball and she is forced to hit the ball, she will have a negative experience.

These all seem very reasonable and manageable in our coaching plans. Number 1 is the ideal situation. This Kristen is ready to go; you are ready to have her go; and everyone is happy. Number 2 happens quite often. This Kristen is ready and able to hit that ball – she wants to hit that ball, but someone or something is standing in her way and she is feeling unhappy about the whole business. (Have you ever sat on the bench, itching to get into the game, and the coach ignored you – he said you weren't ready but you knew you were ready?)

Number 3 is the really scary one and yet you and I see it many times. This is the one that brings out the verbal abuse and the insults. This Kristen is just not able to swing that bat and her coach and/or parents are not willing for that to be O. K. They keep pushing her, abusing her. "You're not even trying." "Are you some kind of sissy?"

They are not willing to wait a little while until Kristen has developed physically to the place that she can do the task. This Kristen has known those traumatic episodes in which Mom and Dad pushed and shoved her to do things and being abusive to her, making her feel guilty or an embarrassment to her family when she wasn't able to do them. "Well, she's six years old and our neighbor's girl is younger than her and look how she can swing that bat."

A Variation on the Readiness Theme

I've often wondered why Thorndike stopped after giving those three laws. In our business, this is a 2 x 2 matrix and there has to be a fourth law, so I will give you:

Pierro's Fourth Law of Readiness

(A Variation on a Theme by Thorndike)

- If Kristen isn't ready to learn how to hit the ball, she will not be forced to hit the ball and that's O.K. and she's O.K.

Here we have reasonable, intelligent, caring coaches and parents who accept Kristen right where she is and deal with her in terms of what she can do and what she can't do. They are the same parents who waited patiently for her to take her first steps, to be able to use the bathroom, to learn to read. I hope you have a lot of this kind of parents in your Pack.

The Coach — A Professional Teacher

Ready or Not – They Are Always Ready

One of the big tasks coaches have is to determine what a player is ready to learn to do in his sport. Then he will be able to teach what is needed in a way that the player can learn with a reasonable amount of success. We can use the term 'maturity' to indicate whether the player has grown to the level needed to perform the tasks that are required.

It's a fact that in most if not all of the issues with which we deal with kids, some kids are ready before others. Well, let's look at some familiar issues – a baby's first steps, for example. There is absolutely nothing that Hazel and Jim can do to have their baby Joy walk one minute before she is physically and neurologically mature enough to walk. Sufficient strength of legs, balance, control of muscles and other factors will determine when she walks. So Joy is physically and neurologically ready to walk at 11 months. Oh, oh! A call from Hazel's sister, Megan. Her daughter, Lois, is only 10 months old and she has just taken her first step.

Is Lois smarter than Joy? Not necessarily. Will she be a better athlete? No one can predict that; in fact some late bloomers can become some of the best athletes. That is, if they don't let their self-image get shot down by a lot of negative messages from coaches and teammates or get cut from teams by coaches and give up. The coaches most apt to cut them down are those who must win so they don't let them play or those who "don't have the time to work with those 'clumsy' kids."

To Cut or Not to Cut?

If Meredith Vieira asks you who the outstanding basketball player of the first half of the 20th Century was and you want to be a Millionaire, you must choose "George Mikan" and make that's your final answer. His story is an inspiration for all those 'clumsy' kids.

Mikan played with the Minneapolis Lakers in the late 1940s. He was 6 feet, 10 inches tall, a standout giant in those days. As a high school student in Joliet, Illinois, and as a freshman at Notre Dame, he had been an unsuccessful overgrown, clumsy

The Coach — A Professional Teacher

youth. In 1943, he enrolled at DePaul University in Chicago under a new coach, Ray Meyer. Coach Meyer also saw an awkward giant trying to play basketball. However he saw something else; this young man had dreams and the determination to work toward them. The Coach, as he became known, spent hours on end working independently with Mikan and the results are in.

Mikan was an All American in 1944, 1945, and 1946. He led DePaul to the championship of the biggest college tournament of that time, the National Invitational Tournament, in 1945. He led the Lakers to 6 titles in the National Basketball Association, he was individual scoring leader for 3 years, he was on the all-star team every year that he played, he was elected to the Naismith Memorial Hall of Fame, and to cap it off, in a special poll taken in 1950, he was named the greatest basketball player in the first half of the 20th century.

That's what a little dedication and hard work can do for you and it does tell us a lot about Ray Meyer and why he was such a successful coach. What if he had cut Mikan from his Blue Demon squad? Would Mikan have gone to another school or would that have been the last in a series of failure messages, the straw that broke the camel's back? I wonder if he ever thought about giving up on himself?

You may want to read about another basketball player; the one voted the best basketball player of the second half of the 20th Century – a fellow by the name of Michael Jordan – and find out how he got along in his high school career.

A Personal Note – I had the privilege of watching Mikan play with the Minneapolis Lakers against the Chicago Stags in Chicago a while back (O.K., a long while back). His defense was great, he owned the boards on both ends of the court, and his hook shot was awesome.

How do you find out if each of your players is ready to play the game? As Dr. Hymes might say, "Kristen is ready to learn how to play ball – it's our job to find out which tasks she is ready to learn and then to teach her in a caring, fun-filled way do." That's simple – not easy, but simple. Every one of your players

The Coach — A Professional Teacher

is ready to learn and perform some aspect of the game – It's our job as coach to find out what each of them is ready to do and then to help them move from where they are to a stronger, more successful place.

The Sneaky Cut

As commissioner of a Bambino baseball league, I became even more aware of a gimmick some coaches used to cut kids from the team. Each team had 14 players, and the rules said that each player had to play one inning in the field and bat at least one time, unless the game was shortened by the 10 run rule.

Some teams began losing players mysteriously. They didn't show up for the practices and then for the games, so as the coaches said, "They cut themselves." Of course they didn't cut themselves. In practices, they were kept busy carrying bat bags and chasing down balls fouled over the backstop and bouncing down the street. If they got to the game, they were put in right field, and everyone knows what that means and they were told when they got to bat to just stand there and not swing – they might get walked. And they heard the coach saying, "Darn, it's the 5th inning and we got to get those guys in." and "Good, we've gotten everyone in; let's get those guys out and put the regulars back in." These are such great boosts to their self-esteems.

The Rug Rats are losing 5-4 in the last of the 7th. There are two outs and Josie has just hit a double and she's standing out at second. Jeri slid into third and is dusting herself off. Coach Jason is jumping up and down in the 3rd base coaching box – and he excitedly turns and he sees Gloria walking toward the plate with a bat in her hand – he just barely stops himself from shouting, "OH, NO," but his facial and body expression says it all. Gloria has a batting average of .125. She gets one hit in every eight at bats. Do you know that Gloria thought that this might be one of those one-in-eight times and then she got that message from Coach Jason . . . ?

You don't think she got that message? You haven't walked a mile in Gloria's spikes.

The Coach — A Professional Teacher

If our purpose in coaching is to win today, then go with the horses. If our purpose is to teach everyone how to play The Game, to learn sportsmanship, to get an appreciation for sports, to build for the future, then we don't cut.

I wish some coaches would be honest and just say, "The only thing that's important to me is for my team to win. That's all that counts. I really don't care about all that other stuff." Then parents could choose to have their kids play for him or go in a different direction.

If we suspect that little Stanley may become another Alex Rodriguez, and that clumsy Gloria may become another Mia Hamm, then we can't cut them. Or maybe they will never become good players but they may become highly successful store owners and because of their happy sports experience they would sponsor a team sometime in the future.

In the end, we must go to our basic beliefs about sports and children and decide which is the most important: Winning the Title, or Developing the Potential of each child on our team. Winning is important – so are Stanley and Gloria. Which comes first? What are our priorities?

Stages of Development

I learned a lesson in maturation and competition in my first year of teaching Kiddy P. E. in Barrington, Illinois. I was in a K-6 school so I had to be creative about my gym setups. One time I had the volleyball net up for the upper grades and, of course, the kindergarten and lower grade kids couldn't play the regular game of volleyball. So, I invented a game for them that I called 'Clean up Your Own Backyard.'

I got out all 15 playground balls and divided the kids into two teams. I put 7 balls at the back wall on each side and held one. I said to the kids, "When I throw this ball into the net, you start throwing all the balls on your side over the net to the other side. Clean up your own backyard. When I blow my whistle, stop." They went to work. They were throwing, chasing down and fielding the balls, and getting good physical activity. Everyone was on his own, scrambling, throwing, chasing, and yelling.

The Coach — A Professional Teacher

When I blew the whistle, they stopped and then – they all simply jumped up and down and hollered. They didn't count how many balls were on each side of the net as I figured they would. The game was over and wasn't it fun!! Which side won? Who cares? Let's do it again!!

One day, the sixth graders were coming into the gym early and the game was still on. "Hey, Mr. Pierro, can we play that game?" several of them asked me and the rest said, "Yeah, how about it? "So I said O.K. and we went at it. The same game? Not on your life – it was a completely different game. We had to choose up sides. The 'leaders' said things like, "You play back and try to catch the balls." "Throw the balls as far back as you can." "Get rid of the balls quick." When I blew the whistle after 5 minutes, action was stopped, and counting began. The winners cheered and the losers said, "Let's play again." Two simple points here:

- Very young children are not concerned about whether they win or lose– the joy is in the playing of the game – "Team" has no meaning to them.
- Older children are more invested in winning but even at that age they understand that in order to win you have to have cooperation among the players.

The Pack is important to the individual Wolves.

Can the Kids enjoy playing the game only if they win? If so, let's quit telling them the Big Lie, "You're going to learn how to play tennis and you're going to have a lot of fun!"

Emotional Readiness

Are your kids emotionally ready to deal with defeat, rejection, stress, verbal abuse, or just plain being hollered at? In fact, are they ready to deal with winning? Can they deal with the highs and lows of the game and the results? There are cases of kids with headaches, upset stomachs, depression, and any number of physical, mental, and emotional distresses as a result of their involvement with sports. They simply are not ready to deal with the game as their coaches and parents expect and want them to be.

Frankly, I think their coaches and/or parents are the ones who are immature, but have we made winning so important to the kids that we have caused their emotional well-being and self-image to be in jeopardy? If so, we have done a terrible injustice to them and to the Game.

Recognizing Uniqueness

One of the things that we are sure of is that each of us is a unique individual; different from every other person who ever lived. We all want to be treated as something special, and certainly each of us is special. We have to keep reminding ourselves however that in dealing with others, in this case, our players, that each of them also is special and wants to be accepted as someone who is special.

Fact #1 every person is unique in many ways – Steve is like no other person.

Fact #2 every person in many ways is the same as every other person – Steve is also the same as every other person in many ways.

These facts confront us as coaches. We try to teach the same thing to everyone and it works – to some extent. We also teach everyone differently according to each one's particular natural movements – and this also works. Everybody is different. We don't all bat the same or run the same or throw the same. Identify and appreciate the natural differences and take advantage of them. You will win more games with players who are becoming the best they can be instead of players who are busy making sure they're doing everything the right way, that is your way.

Just imagine what might have happened if some coach had told Jack Nicklaus that he couldn't let his right elbow "fly" on the back swing, or if someone got hold of Stan Musial when he was young and told him that his "peek around the corner" stance was wrong, or if Evonne Goolagong, the Australian aborigine who became a great tennis champion, had been forced to change her beautiful, flowing movements into more practical choppy steps, or some track coach tried to change

The Coach — A Professional Teacher

Michael Johnson's style because he runs too upright? Our job as coaches is to take our Becky Jones as she is and make her the best Becky Jones that she could possibly become.

The Natural Way Is the Best Way

I have always thought it necessary to have my basketball players dribble, shoot, pass, and so forth, as natural for them as possible. In addition, there were things that I could tell them that would fit into their mode that would improve them. I think we coaches often interfere with the natural movements that our kids have so that we can give them the 'right' moves.

I recall my good friend, Fran. I was playing with a semi-pro baseball team and he was our star pitcher. He had a natural sidearm delivery that was very effective for him and bad news for the opposing batters; especially his good curve against right hand hitters. A few years later, he was picked up by a traveling squad in a larger city. His new coach thought that Fran would be faster and more consistent if he threw three quarter. Well, you know what happened – Fran not only was less effective but he started to have some pains in his pitching arm. This story has a happy ending. Fran got back home and went back to his natural rhythm and his pains left and his fastball and curve came back. If it ain't broke, don't fix it.

Just last week, The Golf Channel had a special program on golf professionals with "strange" swings. Among those shown in action were Jim Furyk, Ray Floyd, Jim Thorpe, Arnold Palmer, Annika Sorenstam, and Nancy Lopez. For an interest analysis of Jim Furyk's swing get on the internet and type in his name.

I am right handed. For my free throw shots, I set my right foot on the center dot on the free throw line and brought my left foot back so that my body was perpendicular to the basket. My Navy coaches and college coaches just let me do it my way – after all, I was doing OK.

Study your players – get to know how they do things in their own natural ways before you start making those changes. And then make the changes only in relation to those natural ways.

The Coach — A Professional Teacher

Uniqueness is not limited to the physical aspects. Each of us has a unique set of behavior traits and patterns. We have had different experiences and have developed different perceptual views of ourselves – each of us sees the world differently. We see success in a very personal way. My measures of success may be a real turnoff for you, as yours may be for me.

Learning Models

The younger the player is or the newer she is to the game, the more it is necessary that she be given first-hand experiences with the skills and knowledge that she'll need. Whether we like it or not, we are not genetically predetermined or neurologically wired to run bases in a counter-clockwise direction. That is a Convention not a Natural issue. It is Learned not Instinctive. The experiences that we initially learn by must be as real, that is, as much like the actual game experience, as possible.

Let's start out with six year old Peggy. She has watched some games but hasn't played yet. Coach Dundee has her hit the ball off the tee and he tells her, "Run to first base." (Oral Direction). She gets there O.K. He says, "Now, go to second base." Oh, Oh! Cognitive overload. Peggy thinks, "I'm here on first base and I don't know where second base is." So Coach Dundee goes down to Peggy, points to second base, turns her shoulders in that direction says "Go there" and gives her a little push to start her on her way. She gets to second base and stops. Now her next problem is, "Where do I go from here?" So Coach Dundee trots down to second base... And this will continue as long as she uses only oral direction.

Meanwhile, Coach Adams, over on the other diamond, has her young charges standing with her at home plate. She has Janice, her young, high school age assistant, helping her. "O. K. kids, Janice is going to run the bases. Watch her run and I'll tell you what she's doing." (Janice trots down to first base – Demonstration) Janice is running down to first base and Coach Adams is giving Oral Directions) Now she is running to second base and now to third base and now here she comes home. "All right, now I want you five girls to follow Janice while she runs the bases again. (And they start off) Now, you five girls go with Coach Webb. Great! And now the rest of you come along with me." (Personal Experience)

Coach Adams is starting her kids off with actual experience and then she can use all the other techniques in a very meaningful (to the kids) way. We don't in any way try to separate these learning strategies. One flows naturally into another and that's how it should be. They add to one another and they reinforce one another.

The more concrete the experience is, the more the player is involved in the action, the easier the learning is and the more permanent it will be.

The Learning Modalities

There are four major learning modalities that each of us uses to learn about the world around us:

Visual – by what we see.

Auditory – by what we hear.

Kinesthetic – by our body movements – in action.

Tactile – by what we physically feel by touch.

We are all Visual, Auditory, Kinesthetic, and Tactile learners and we apply them in different degrees. At the same time, we have a primary modality by which we learn best while the other modalities are being utilized at a lesser extent. For Vera the Visual, most of what she learns is through her eyes (Visual), some through her ears (Auditory), and just a little through body movements (Kinesthetic). Annie the Auditory is mostly Auditory, some Kinesthetic, and very little Visual. Kerry the Kinesthetic is mainly Kinesthetic, almost as much Visual, and almost no Auditory. Tactile seems to be lesser used in learning except that in sports 'feel' means a lot at the performance level.

Just be aware that Vera, the visual one, may not remember the exact words that you use while Annie, the aural one, remembers every word. Kerry, the kinesthetic one, is watching for you to make your moves. In the same manner, Vera packs away a mental image of what you did and how you did it (or she may form a mental image of what you said). Annie needs some action to go with the words and Kerry is still waiting for you to do something so that he can copy you.

The best way to learn something new is Experiential – yep, learn by doing, because all of the senses are involved. This is why the best way to learn how to play soccer is to get on the field and kick the ball around with a team and against another team. This is also why a player doesn't learn a lot by sitting on the bench watching others doing it. The next best way to learn is by Visualizing – using the camera we have in our heads. A strong visualization of an action is almost as effective as the action itself. Another is by use of a Demonstration – using our actions so that our players can form a visual memory of what you want them to learn. Another is drawing a Diagram – if the player is a visual learner as most of us are, this works very well.

Another is by the use of Oral Directions – if the player is an oral learner as some of us are. If you have a musician on the team, oral and kinesthetic are really good. Of course with athletics, Kinesthetic Learning is always available and appropriate.

The point here is that you should make use of techniques that use all of these modalities. For example, draw a diagram on your clipboard while you are giving oral directions and then demonstrate the action.

Sandy's Models

Let's get back to Sandy and his learning his basketball skills. Coach Haley says, "Sandy, we use the fast break. When the ball is rebounded on your side of the court, you move out over there so you can get the outlet pass." (Verbal Directions)

He observes the blank expression on Sandy's face so he gets out his clip board and draws this (Visual Diagram).

The Coach — A Professional Teacher

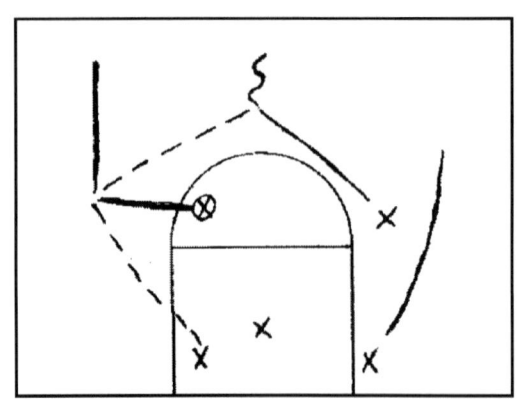

"This is you here – the X with a circle around it. When the ball is rebounded on your side of the court, you move out over here so you can be clear to get the outlet pass." (Verbal Information)

Sandy says, "O.K., is that an exact spot?" Coach Haley clarifies the task, "You have to be pretty close to that spot so the rebounder doesn't have to look for you. Now stand here and I'll take a shot and Art will rebound it and get it out to you at that spot." (Simulation - Experiential) He takes a shot, Amy rebounds it and clears it Sandy who has moved into the correct position. "O.K. Good job. Let's try it again. This time, Art will give it to you so that you're on the move when you get it. (Verbal Affirmation and Verbal Directions) O.K., Art, let's do it."

Coach Haley has them run through it a couple of more times, changing the positions that Art rebounds the shots. "Dave, take the other guard spot. Sandy, look at this diagram again. When you get the outlet pass, get it to Dave who will take the center lane and you go down the left lane." (Higher Level Simulation)

After several attempts, "Good, now Sandy, I'm going to have the ball go to the other side of the court. What are you going to do?" "I'll go to the middle of the court, get the pass from Heather and take the center lane." "Right, we'll be working on the rest of the break in a while."

(In this instance, Sandy is me on my Junior College basketball team. I am basically visual. Coach Strell kept hollering at me

122

for not getting it. Finally, he drew it out on his clip board and I got it.)

Our Senses in Action

As we run down the soccer field, we see the ball as it is intercepted by Ted, one of our team mates, we hear the ball as it strikes his chest, we see the ball as it is passed to us, we feel the ball as it meets the toe of our shoe, we look up and see Ted making a cut to get a return pass, we visualize the ball traveling from our foot to his foot, we and we see the ball as it's picked up by Ted's shoe.

We learn how to do these actions and use all of these senses and after a while we don't notice them – and that's good. In the learning stages, however, we have to focus on each of these skills until it becomes 'second nature,' 'automatic,' and 'unconscious.'

Motivating Yourself

Self-motivation and motivating other people are very different operations. Let's look at self-motivation because we can't motivate other people unless we are motivated ourselves. Motivation is one of the great builders in our lives. It is concerned mainly with the whys behind our actions and activities:

- Why do I want to be a coach?
- Why do I want my players to be good sportsmen?

Ordinarily, our motivation comes from our dreams or our needs. You may say, "I want to be a coach because I have always wanted to be a positive factor in the lives of young people" or "I want to be a coach because I like to strive for excellence and coaching will give me the opportunity to do that." You have set becoming a coach as a goal and you are motivated into goal seeking activity. You focus so strongly on reaching your goal that there is no room for thoughts of failure. Obstacles are what you see when you take your eyes off your goals.

The reaching of the goal is an important part of the process, but the journey, the striving for that goal is where the joy and the sense of worth is. As you are reaching your goal, you set up a new, more rewarding goal because the journey toward self-realization and the achieving of excellence are the real goals in the life of a growing, successful person; the real goals in your life.

The Motivating Coach

Is Coach Doakes of our Falcons team a good motivator of others? An indirect way of considering this is to examine her ability to inspire her players. She is an excellent model. She inspires them to be their best. She cares deeply about her players and she cares about herself and her own dreams and aspirations. She knows that we motivate and we inspire others only when we, ourselves, care enough to do whatever is necessary to reach our own dreams. She wants her players to experience the joy of playing the game. She knows that and she does whatever it takes to get it done.

We motivate and we inspire others only when we, ourselves, care enough to do whatever is necessary to reach our own dreams.

Chapter 4 Planning For Success

Rights and Responsibilities

Winning Strategies

Goal Setting and Success

Winning and Competition

Empowering Communication

Planning for Success

My Players'	
Rights	**Responsibilities**
The right to be treated fairly.	The responsibility to treat others fairly.
. The right to express my ideas and to be heard.	The responsibility to listen to others and respect their ideas.
The right to participate.	The responsibility to do my best.
The right to have good coaching.	The responsibility to cooperate with my coaches.
The right to be safe.	The responsibility to follow safety rules.
The right to be treated with respect.	The responsibility to treat teammates, coaches, opponents, and officials with respect.
The right to have my equipment safe from loss or damage.	The responsibility to leave other players' property alone unless I have their permission.
The right to share in making decisions for the team.	The responsibility to think and act in a responsible way.
The right to play and not be cut.	The responsibility to attend practices.
The right to be a member of the team	The responsibility to be a trustworthy team member.
The right to have and use good equipment.	e responsibility to take care of my and team's equipment.
The right not to be insulted or embarrassed.	The responsibility to respect the feelings of others.
THE RIGHT TO EXPERIENCE THE JOY OF PLAYING THE GAME.	**THE RESPONSIBILITY TO MAKE THE BEST OF MY EXPERIENCE.**

Planning for Success

Players' Rights and Responsibilities

On the facing page are the Players' Rights and Responsibilities. This can be the basis for the goals that you and your players will create. This list includes performance, behavioral, and attitude goals. You can present this to the players at the beginning of the season and go over each of the items in detail. During the year, you may review the items to keep them fresh in the players' minds. In the player handbook, these are written in the first person – My Rights and Responsibilities.

You can also use R and R for individual cases. Remind them that they signed a contract with you and that you will live by the contract and expect them to do likewise.

The Case of Otto the Outsider

Otto has just joined your team this year and he's a good player; an asset to the team, a good skater and passer. Early in the pre-season practices, however, you notice that the other players don't let him get cozy with them – in fact, they go out of their way to avoid him. When he makes a good play there are few if any high fives. It's time to check it out. Who shall I talk to? Let's try Coach Lowe. "Say, Pat, what's with the guys' attitudes toward Otto?"

"Well, Coach, Otto's family just moved into the Maple Crest Apartments and he attends Madison School." Oh, oh, he lives

Planning for Success

on the East side of town in the government housing and attends that at-risk school. He doesn't 'belong' with the middle-class Titans.

Oh, I see the signs now – Otto's skates are scuffed up, obviously hand-me-downs or purchased at Goodwill, and his accent shows that "He's not from around here."

What to do:

If this were a fiction story, Otto would have scored the winning goal to beat the Broncos and win the league championship, the players would carry him off the ice without caring where he lives or what he wears or where he goes to school or how he talks.

You have held sessions on the Players' Rights and Responsibilities but something didn't take. O.K., it's time to call a special meeting – right now. At this time be general in your message – you can get specific in individual cases if necessary. "Guys, we need to review one of your rights and responsibilities on this team. The 10th Right says: "The right to be a member of the team" and the corresponding Responsibility says: "The responsibility to be a reliable, trustworthy team member."

"This means that each and every one of you is a rightful, qualified member of this team – you all belong here – there are no exceptions. Coach Lowe, Coach Washington, and I have no pets or favorites and we have nobody who is being treated as being less of a person than anyone else. This means that no one is treated poorly because he or she is a different color, comes from a different neighborhood, talks differently, dresses differently, or any other comparison you may want to make."

"You may be tired of the Wolf and the Pack idea but you're going to hear it all season long. This team is a Pack and each of you is a Wolf who belongs to the Pack. Every person on this team is equal in our eyes, all our eyes – not just the coaches. I want you to keep this message in your head – Everyone belongs on this team simply because he or she is a member of this team. There is no other requirement – and you're going to treat everyone on this team as your teammate." Remind them

Planning for Success

again that they signed a contract with you and that you will live by the contract and expect them to do likewise.

If this persists with some of the guys, you have to get personal and tougher with them, e.g., "No problem – If you can't work with Otto, we'll be glad to help you get traded to another team."

There are no personal attributes that can or should keep us from building strong, caring individuals and a strong team that nurtures each of its players at the same level.

Using *R and R* in Individual Cases

Terry has just struck out and thrown his bat to the backstop. "That stupid umpire doesn't know where the darned strike zone is!" Coach Sara Garcia, who believes in taking good care of equipment, in safety, and in natural consequences (let the punishment fit the crime), says, "Terry, since you threw that bat and could have hurt someone, you won't be able to use that bat again until you have a session on bat safety with me. We can do that at our next practice. In the meantime read #5 and #11 in *"My Rights and Responsibilities."*

This means that **Terry** made a decision that resulted in his sitting on the bench for the rest of the game. Note that Coach Garcia didn't say. "Terry, you're out of this game because you threw the bat" which would mean that **she** had made the decision.

Winning Strategies
Strategy #1 – Good Coaches Enjoy Their Players and Enjoy the Game

You really can identify the good coach quickly. She is out there with the kids; enjoying them, enjoying the game. Her practices are fun to watch. As you watch, you are aware of the lack of stress. In place of stress is intensity – working hard on skills and strategies. There is a lot of activity and you can see some challenges being thrown out to the players – some fun competitions.

During the game, she is intense. She has high expectations and demands focus and alertness from the players. She is always very positive, "Way to stand in there." "Nice catch." "Way to

Planning for Success

back up the catcher." "Good eye." She doesn't throw compliments around – when you get one, it means something and the players respond with energy and purpose. Sometimes she's appropriately demanding. "Where were you on that rundown? You need to help Paul out on that play" but she is never demeaning, sarcastic, or insulting.

I believe that the calm, firm, positive expecting coach is much more effective and wins a lot more games than the loud, abusive, hard-nosed coach. In her own way she is just as intense and a much stronger person.

Strategy #2 – Good Coaches Deal With the Whole Player

Good coaches are aware that their players are whole human beings. Besides being athletic persons, they are mental, social, emotional, esthetic, school, and family persons. There are times when other parts of their lives are having a strong effect on them and they just can't focus all of their energy and attention on the game or on practice. We have to respect and honor the other parts of their lives and keep the game in perspective.

Remember: In the final analysis, it's a game and only a game.

Strategy #3 – Good Coaches Set Behavior Goals with Their Players

Children, that is you and me and everyone else, have goals that determine their behavior. A wise mentor of mine told me to learn Child Psychology so that I could better understand people of all ages – including the parents of my players.

Strategy #4 – Good Coaches Create Respect for One Another

Positive coaches respect their players and thereby they're respected by their players – the goal is mutual respect. I hope I didn't hear you say, "They may not like me, but they're going to respect me."

Fear is not the same as respect – you get respect the hard way; you earn it.

Planning for Success

Strategy #5 – Good Coaches Teach and Use Cooperation

Positive coaches believe in competition but that comes only after they have built up a great sense of cooperation. First you play with your teammates, and then you play against the opponents.

Strategy #6 – Good Coaches Coach With Positive Expectancy

Good coaches expect things to work out well and communicate this to their players. We get what we expect to get. If you expect Larry to give you trouble; you got it. If you expect Larry to be O. K.; you have a chance to be right.

Strategy #7 – Good Coaches Relate To Their Players' Needs

In order to have a good self-concept, there are needs that all of us must have attended to and fulfilled. Here are the needs of kids:

- Self-identity – Recognition
- Belonging to a Community (Your Team)
- Power/Input
- Success Experiences
- Knowledge of Their Growth

Strategy #8 – Good Coaches Set Performance Goals with Their Players Your players must have some input in their goals – they must have some ownership their own. They will work harder to attain them if they're involved in selecting their personal and team goals. Setting goals keeps us focused and helps us stay on course.

If you don't set goals and know where you're going, you'll probably end up somewhere else. Anonymous

Strategy #9 – Good Coaches Recognize Individual Uniqueness

One of the things that we are sure of is that each of us is a unique individual; different from every other person who ever lived. We all want to be treated as something special – and certainly each of us is special.

Planning for Success

Strategy #10 – Good Coaches Recognize Different Patterns of Behavior

There are patterns of behavior that all of us adopt in order to be able to deal with the world. Sometimes we want to reach a goal to accomplish something that is important to us. Sometimes we have to protect ourselves from pain or embarrassment. Sometimes we need to be noticed and affirmed by peers and adults. Sometimes we need to get away from other people or from painful circumstances. Sometimes we need to be able to take control of some part of our lives.

To do that we are apt to become Whiners or Clowns or Pests or whatever best suits our needs. A good, caring mentor/coach can help us find healthy, productive ways to reach our goals so that we won't need to play the games that are hindering our growth and hurting our team effort.

Planning for Success

Goal Setting and Success
Players Rights and Responsibilities

The Players' Rights and Responsibilities can be the basis for the goals that you and your players will create.

The Team - Working and Playing Together

Sometime in the future, people will be looking at our culture and will find that the best examples of team work – group goal setting and achievement – were in our team sports ventures. In team sports, it is essential that we first have cooperation among all elements of the team and then we'll be able to compete at a much higher level against our opponents – in team sports, cooperation always precedes competition.

Goals are organized plans that define the directions and the levels of achievement that we hope to reach. They provide purpose for our activity and give it direction. Without goals our efforts would tend to wander. We wouldn't think of beginning a long trip without first knowing where we planned to go. Likewise, we will plan our athletic program with a set of goals by which we can determine how far we have come and how far we still have to go. Goals keep us from going off our planned course.

Team; a Set of Individuals with Common Goals

Your team is more than a collection of individuals – it has a system of relationships among its players and coaches. You, your assistants, and your players form one unit which you call the Eagles or the Lobos or the Aces. This unit must have a set of goals that is agreed upon by the individual members. Without this set of goals, you have a group of individuals; with this set of goals, you will have a team. It is also important that each of your players and coaches has his own set of goals which are in agreement with the goals of the team.

In team sports, cooperation always precedes competition.

Goal Setting Principles

Your goals must be challenging, ones that demand a great deal of effort and dedication on your part and on the part of your players. Unless your goals really challenge you and make you work, you won't improve; you will not be any better for having reached them.

Your goals must be realistic. If your team went 0-14 last year it would be rather unrealistic for you to set a team goal for a 14-0 season. Study the abilities of your team carefully and discuss them with your players who then can help you establish challenging but realistic goals. "Our team is a lot better this year. We are having a winning season."

New and higher goals will be set before you reach the old ones. When your team is well on its way to reaching one of your goals set a new and higher goal. For example, if you set a goal for a winning season (8 - 6 would be a winning season) and you are now 6-3, set a higher standard. "We are making the playoffs." Reaching a goal without having a new one to go after is a good way to "get stuck."

Setting Team Goals – The Process

This goal setting process must be done early in the season, preferably after a few practice sessions and before the season begins.

Here is an overview of the team goal setting process:

1. The coaches will approach the process with Positive Expectancy.
2. The coaches and the players will choose an acceptable list of goals.
3. All members of the team will affirm these goals.
4. These goals will be the basis for self-motivation and team motivation.
5. The reaching of these goals will be the marks of success.

Planning for Success

Step 1. Positive Expectancy

The Coaches will enter into all of their activities with Positive Expectancy, the belief that the situation will work out the way they would like it to. They don't allow any other thoughts to enter their minds. If they allow doubt to enter their minds, the doubt becomes their expectancy and they will end up where they don't want to be.

Head Coach's Affirmation:

"My assistants, my players, and I are having an excellent meeting. We are making good decisions and are laying the foundation for a great year."

Step 2. Creating the Goals

Ask for volunteers to give their goals and put them on large newsprint and as the pages fill up tear them off the pad and tape them to the wall. Personally, I would make sure to include "the joy of being associated with this game" as one of the goals. Use "Fun of playing the game" if "Joy" doesn't express your feelings.

Make sure that all of your goals are listed including character goals and behavior goals. This is a good time to talk about working hard, caring for your teammates, being good sportsmen, and all of the other values that you hold about The Game and how it should be played.

Ask your assistant coaches and the players to choose the goals that all of them could subscribe to, such as, To have a winning season; To spend time with good friends; To learn more about the game; To learn sportsmanship. Don't hesitate to get your own goals for the team up there and to promote them in a reasonable way; after all, you're a member of the team.

The Commitment – Write the agreed upon goals on one large sheet. Now comes the commitment process. Present them to the group prefaced with, "O.K., let's take these one at a time. The first is to have a winning season. Do we all agree on that one?" Go for total agreement. If they all can't agree on a goal, mark it with a question mark and save it for consideration at another time. "We all agree that we want to have a winning

Planning for Success

season. Let's look at the next one." Total agreement on goals unifies the team.

The list that you now have is the basis for your team actually being a team. You have the permission of the group to lead them in the direction that is available and acceptable. You can use these goals for both self-motivation, individual player motivation, and team motivation.

If we allow doubt to enter our minds, the doubt becomes our expectancy and we will end up where we don't want to be.

Step 3. Affirmation of Goals

Write an affirmation for each of these goals. Rewrite the goals in positive terms, first person plural (for the team), present tense.

"We will have a winning season" becomes "We are a winning team and we are having a very successful season."

Before the next practice have these affirmations typed up and copied so that you can give a copy to each player.

Step 4. Motivating Your Players

Coaches can motivate their team any of five basic ways. The first four are external systems – the motivation comes from outside the player. The last one is internal – the motivation comes from the player herself.

We all have had experience with the first two; The Stick and The Carrot.

"The Stick" approach – the use of fear, threats, and punishment to change the efforts or behavior of the player.

"Linda, you didn't get a hit today. If you don't get with it, LouAnn is going to take over."

It is not only negative, it is usually counter-productive. Basically, it is most likely that Linda will tense up and perform more poorly as a result. This will then give the coach more opportunity to threaten and the cycle continues going down.

Planning for Success

*Linda must change her goal from **wanting to** get a hit and enjoying the feeling of accomplishment to **having to** get a hit to avoid losing a place in the lineup.*

Fear also does some terrible things to the team building process. It causes people to worry and to attach that worry to their feelings about their team. It interferes with the open, honest communication that a team demands. It is hard to answer your coach honestly if you're afraid that he may make your response a reason to lay a disciplinary action on you.

The 'Carrot' approach. In Psych 101 you learned about Pavlov's dogs that salivated and barked when they heard their food dishes being filled which then led on to Thorndike's cats and Skinner's pigeons. When the animal does what the researcher wants it to do, it's rewarded. This learning system is called Behavior Modification.

"Anybody who goes 2 for 4 or better gets a sticker on his batting helmet."

Again, the goal is changed – Linda must change her focus on her hitting goals. She has to fit the new goal, to get a sticker, into her goal which was to improve her hitting in order to deal with the coach's goal. Her goal of improving her hitting is confused by a new desire; to acquire a sticker.

Note that this is based on what the researcher (teacher - coach) wants – not necessarily in the best interest of the learner/ player.

Kids are really smart in dealing with this technique and working the system. Linda and the other players will begin expecting a payoff on every accomplishment, for example;

"I've never been late for practice, Coach – don't I get a sticker for that?"

"Hey, Coach, what do we get if we go through practice without complaining?"

Up pops the expectation by the players that they are to be rewarded for doing the things that they are supposed to do. Being on time for practice is expected behavior. Practicing correctly is expected behavior. You are not rewarded for doing

Planning for Success

what you are supposed to do. Practicing and learning to play and enjoy the game is its own reward. When you hang a carrot out there, you have diminished the game and its value.

The Reward System is significantly different because the reward is given without the player asking for it or expecting it. The goal, to play and enjoy the game, stays in place. Luis has had a good day on the track – his start has really improved and he is happy about his accomplishment. You call him aside and say, "Luis, all of your hard work is paying off and I want to tell you how much I admire your energy and spirit."

This is a verbal reward. If you want to augment it with a sticker, that's your call. You could also add to this by giving the reward to him in the presence of the team.

Inspiration is the fourth type of motivation. The coach and his assistants are always acting honestly and with a lot of class. They have high expectations of their own actions. They stay

Planning for Success

positive and deal with the umpires, the crowd, parents, and, of course, their players with genuine courtesy. Linda and her teammates are impressed with the coaches, both in terms of who they are and in what they do, and they are willing and eager to become part of this high class operation.

This is the motivation that you want to create – everything else will work if you have this.

Coaches are Teachers and Teachers are Coaches

You remember Miss Rinehart, don't you? She was that fantastic music teacher everyone loved. She loved music she loved teaching, and she loved her students. She was always there with a smile and encouraging words. And you and your friends sang better than you knew how at the assemblies. You did that for her and also for yourself; you wouldn't have allowed it to be any other way.

Can everyone be an inspiring coach? Of course.

The fifth type of motivation, Accomplishment, is internal – it's self-motivation. Linda has set a goal that she wants to achieve for herself and she is striving to reach it. It has to do with her attitudes and perceptions. As she reaches her goals, she feels better about herself and the game. This is the hallmark of her achieving success. It's an internal process and it's all hers.

Step 5. Goals Achieved and Success

An excellent definition of success is the reaching of goals that you have set for yourself.

As your players reach the goals that they have listed in their journal, give them the recognition that they've earned. A written note, an emblem, a pat on the back, a comment during a debriefing meeting, a call to parents; whatever fits the situation.

You must do that for yourself also. Rewarding yourself for personal accomplishments is a great self-image builder – and you deserve it. You can also share these accomplished goals with your players.

Visualize Your Goals

Another aid to motivation is the technique of visualization. For now it is sufficient to say that you must learn to see your goal in front of you if you want to reach it. It is easier to exert that extra kick when you can see the finish line or goal line ahead of you – even while it is still around the curve. The more clearly you can visualize your goals, the more your desire will inspire you to greater effort.

Visualize your goals, and visualize yourself reaching them. Picture yourself holding the trophy. Picture yourself handing out medals to your kids. Picture yourself fulfilling your goals, and you will be even more motivated to reach them.

Never Lose Sight of Your Major Goal

The realization of your ultimate goals will not come easy. As a result, it is critical that you always keep those major goals in sight. Never forget what you are striving for. If you lose sight of them, you will become less motivated and find yourself putting forth less effort than you should. It is easy to grow discouraged and give up unless you remember your dream and how good you will feel when it becomes a reality. It is also easy to spend too much time looking back on your past successes before you have reached your major goal; once you begin to feel satisfied with your achievements in the past, you lose sight of your objective; never look back until you have reached all of your goals.

Positive Personal Goals

As with all people, your players have some goals that are natural and exist in all groups. Here is how these goals could be stated:

Acknowledgment – I want to be acknowledged for what I do and for who I am – give me a pat on the back, a smile, a 'nice job', a nod, any action to let me know that you know that I exist and that you care about me – about who I am – not just about what I do on the field.

Planning for Success

Acceptance/Belonging – I want to be a member of your team - I want to belong to something worthwhile. I qualify for membership simply by being on the team – I belong.

Justice (Fairness) – I want to be treated as an individual person and to know that I will be on an equal basis with everyone else on the team. I want to trust you – that you will be fair to me and to everyone else. I will respond by being fair to you; by trusting you.

Involvement/Contribution – I want to be a contributing member of this team and I will help make this team become the best that it can be in every way that I can.

Autonomy – I want to be heard when I have something important to say. I want to help this team by giving positive, helpful, suggestions.

Community – I want to belong to a positive, caring peer group – to be a member of a great community. I am willing to be a responsible, contributing member.

Accomplishment/Success – I want to be a success. Success for me is doing my very best to achieve the goals I've set for myself as an individual player and as a team member.

Winning and Competition

Let's get to these two most critical concerns we have to deal with in coaching kids and dealing with their parents.

Winning

"Winning isn't everything; It's the only thing." Vince Lombardi is quoted (or misquoted) as saying. And in the context of his job, this is probably a true statement. He was a professional coach and the one and only criterion for success at that level is winning.

In one of the biographical books written about Joe Paterno, he comments on this issue. He was offered the coaching job with a National Football League team and he declined to take it. He was offered a lot more money and he was going to have front office power to go along with the coaching. He really struggled

Planning for Success

with making the decision but, of course, we know that he stayed at Penn State.

Why would he stay at Penn State instead of taking a job almost every other college coach would give an eye tooth for? According to Coach Paterno, he wanted to stay at Penn State because of the benefits he got over and above winning games. What were those benefits? Number 1 was that his players were really student/athletes. The rate of his players graduating from college is much higher than the average. When he was asked which of his teams was the greatest, he replied that he would know 20 years down the line when he knew what they had accomplished in the future as a result of what he had done with them while they were his charges.

"Winning Isn't Everything."

I have heard that said so many times by coaches and parents associated with youth sports. This statement begs for an answer to a question that we absolutely have to ask. This question pertains to everyone up to the professional ranks where winning really is everything. So let's explore this puzzle – "Winning isn't everything."

It isn't? Well, if it isn't, what else is there? If you attend one of my clinics I will have you write your responses and then share them with the group. Since you aren't at one of clinics, let me supply some of the answers that I have heard:

The Kids will learn to enjoy playing and practicing.

The Kids will learn the rules and history of the game.

The Kids will learn more about responsibility.

The Kids will learn what good sportsmanship is and will act accordingly.

The Kids will learn to have respect for their teammates, their opponents, their Coaches, and the Officials on the field.

The Kids will learn how to compete fairly and honestly.

The Kids will learn good teamwork and cooperation.

The Kids will learn that sitting on the bench is sometimes the role that we must play in being a good team member.

Planning for Success

The Kids will learn to appreciate the game.

The Kids will learn that hard work pays off.

The Kids will learn how to win gracefully.

The Kids will learn how to deal with their losses.

The Kids will learn how to put the needs of the team and their own personal needs into the correct perspective.

The Kids will learn that when they do their very best, their Coaches and Parents will appreciate them for who they are and for what they do.

Above all, The Kids will be experiencing the joy of playing The Great Game; whatever that game may be.

Now that we have listed our What Else Is There? concerns, the next question is "Now that we know what else there is, what are we going to do about it?" It seems to me that we have the road map and it's up to us to do the traveling.

We have really lost if we don't grow simply from the experience of having played the game.

"I really love this game."

I Played My Heart Out, Isn't That Good Enough?

I have never understood how a Player, including myself, could feel bad or be made to feel bad by someone about having competed at his very best and having experienced the playing of a great game simply because we lost the game. If that's what we took from the game, we have missed this opportunity for improving ourselves for the next game; for the next life challenge; for our personal growth for the rest of our lives.

What did I learn about myself from this game, whether we won or lost? What did I learn about myself in relation to other people from this game, whether we won or lost? What did I learn about life from this game, whether we won or lost?

"I'm A Winner." Really, in Everything You Do?

I had a player I'll call Doug Meddors whose father wouldn't accept anything but that his 12 year old son would be a perfect player and the star of the team, league, nation, and universe. I later thought wouldn't it be interesting if Doug challenged his dad to play a computer game and Doug beat him every time? How many times would Mr. Meddors lose before he said, "Oh, this game is ridiculous and I'm not going to play anymore?"

Who Wants To Be A Loser - Loser - Loser?

Of all the present day golfers; I like Jim Furyk best. I think it's his intensity and his ability to keep on task regardless of what happens that I like. I would love to play a round with him some day. And, of course, he would beat me (that is, unless he spotted me about 20 strokes).

What I would not like is to be forced to play against him every week with no strokes and some of my money on the line and lose and then have "Furyk Wallops Pierro Again" broadcast all over the media. Not only my money but my self-image would take a beating and it wouldn't be long before I said, "I'm out of here."

Am I that much different from the Kids on your team? Don't they lay their self-images on the line every game?

Take calculated risks - don't take the failures personally - it's all part of the learning process to get you to your goal.

Competition
Fair and Honest Competition

There are a lot of myths about what competition is and what it does for us and to us. It is especially critical when we are dealing with young kids. Competition for kids is different from competition among adults and it should be. How we make adjustments for competition is crucial for both kids and adults.

Fair Competition means that everyone in the game has the possibility of winning.

Adjusting the Competition

When I was coaching basketball in a small high school basketball in northern Illinois, there was only one class of teams. We all competed for one State Champion. When we got into the Regional and Sectional Tournaments, we played against schools that were a lot larger than us. Fair competition was judged to be every school against every other school regardless of size. Obviously, as borne out by the records, larger schools with a bigger player base, experienced coaches, better gyms, and more resources were winning almost all of the state championships.

Since that time there have been some adjustments in many states in the name of Fair Competition – so little Mason High School no longer competes with the large city and suburban high schools for the one and only state title. Most states have from two to six levels and two to six high school champions.

I think that's fair, don't you? I think it's great that a team from some little town in whatever state can say, "We're #1," despite the fact that it probably wouldn't have a chance in a series of tournament games against big city schools with ten times as many students to choose from, full-time coaches, up to date equipment, etc.

Planning for Success

No one seems to question the right of students from a small school to wave their index fingers and shout, *"We're #1!"* Isn't that great?

Competition in Adults' Sports

We adults talk about having to compete in the "Real World" and yet we are very clear about when and how we are going to compete. There are some very distinct rules that must be followed and here they are expressed in the form of models:

Model #1 - The Big League Model

This is the model, the only model most people have in mind when they talk about Competition. This is the model that is used effectively to produce professional athletes. We continually promote the good players and cut the poor players. The best of the good players play; the rest sit on the bench or get "cut." This works fine for the professional level. The question is how far down the ladder do we use this model? Jr. High football? – 4th grade basketball? – 6 year old gymnastics? – T-Ball?

Model #2 - The Flight Model

This is the model I described above in my high school. Here are some other uses: Each year many golf and tennis clubs have championship matches. Some of them set up 'flights'. The best 12 players are in the Championship Flight, the next 12 are in the First Flight, the next 12 are in the Second Flight, and so on until all members of the club are included and everyone is competing at a level at which he can win - everyone can be a winner. This is the model that's used in high schools and also in colleges. We have different divisions in the NCAA and the NAIA.

Model #3 - The Handicapping Model

The team I bowled on a few years ago was in a league that uses handicaps. If my team averaged 750 and yours averaged 780, you had to give me a 'spot' or 'handicap'. Usually this is 2/3 of the difference, so your team gave my team a 20 pin spot per game. This made the competition 'fairer' than would a head-to-head contest – each team had a chance to win.

Planning for Success

An Inquiry – I've played golf with some strong 'competitors' – Here's what happens on the first tee:

Me: Let's play for a quarter a hole. (I'm a real gambler) Him: O.K. My handicap is 18, what's yours?

Me: 14 – I give you a stroke on the 3rd, 6th, 11th, and 15th holes.

That settles that – everyone is pleased about the arrangement and we can tee off – the poorer player has a better chance to be a winner.

Observation – *Why should I give him strokes? If he can't measure up, that's his problem.*

Two Non-Competitive Models That Everyone Likes

There are two other models that seem very likely to bring success to the participants. They are non-competitive in comparison to how we usually define competition in sports yet everyone seems to like them. No one gets bent out of shape because winning has other definitions than beating your opponent. Everyone can be and is a winner and is successful. Besides success, these models are the embodiment of the joy of competing and that winning really isn't the only thing.

Model #4 - The Road Race Model.

Anyone who wants can enter – no one is eliminated. Each participant is successful or unsuccessful according to his or her own goals and according to their individual abilities. The major concern for most participants is their PR, Personal Record. Yes, there are real winners and prize money and medals and trophies but those are for a small minority of the participants.

Winning doesn't always entail beating an opponent.

Model #5 - The Special Olympics Model

The Special Olympic philosophy respects each person regardless of his/her disability. When you watch a Special

Planning for Success

Olympics, you see each child doing his best in whatever event he has chosen. Each contestant is acknowledged for his efforts.

Everyone is a winner - winning is the reward for risking and participating.

Cooperation; the Partner of Competition

I have some problems with stickers and other ways of rewarding good performances by an individual player in a team sport. I simply do not want my basketball players competing with each other for high scorer of the game or most assists (I don't want a player to pass up an assist so that he can try to raise his scoring). I want them to work together so that the player with the best opportunity takes the shot.

My wife, Bobbie, played French horn in two symphony orchestras and some other top-level groups and we talk a lot about the differences and similarities of her experiences and my experiences playing and coaching various sports. We agree on one thing without any reservations; the players must cooperate completely in order for the organization to be successful.

The essence of cooperation is in having people working together toward predetermined goals. Whenever we do this it is essential that the individuals involved communicate openly and clearly with one another. They must work cooperatively; they can't get into the trap of hiding their discoveries or ideas so that they will be one-up on their associates. If they do, the whole project is in jeopardy.

Can you imagine the string section of the orchestra competing with the woodwinds?

Competition within the Team

In order to win (that is, to compete successfully), players must cooperate fully – it is often called Teamwork. In my first coaching assignment I was involved in a situation in which competition among players back-fired to the detriment of the team. I had just taken the position of assistant basketball coach along with a new head coach at a high school that was rightfully famous for its great teams.

Planning for Success

I had watched them play several games the year before including when they lost a tough game in the finals of the sectional tournament. They were doing quite well the first half mainly by getting the ball in to their excellent center and he was scoring almost at will. In the second half, the ball wasn't getting to him and the guards were taking most of the shots. They were not hitting too well and the opponents took the lead. Toward the end of the game, the guards started getting back to the center but he had turned "cold" and the time ran out. I remember wondering, "Why isn't that terrific center getting the ball? They should be winning this game."

At halftime in the first game the following year, I was taking the shot charts and score book to the dressing room when one of the guards (who had been in that final game) asked me how many points he had scored. I blinked, said, "I won't tell you" and moved on. The other guard, who had also been in that game, stopped me and asked the same question and got the same answer. Then the light came on — the former coach had set up a competitive system. The top scorer each game and ongoing throughout the season was rewarded. So, when the center started putting up big numbers, each of the guards said, "Wait a minute - it's my turn to catch up" and the game went down the drain. The attitude of these guards probably was built fairly solidly into their subconscious mind and they may not have realized the significance of their behavior in that sectional game.

Regardless, in this case, when individual competition came into the picture, it destroyed cooperation (teamwork) and negatively affected the competition with their opponents. You can be sure that that competitive, reward model was discontinued

Praise and Encouragement

Often I hear coaches saying, "You have to praise your kids" or "We don't praise our kids enough." It's a great idea when done right and can be a trap for both coach and player if done wrong. We like to acknowledge kids for their efforts, but sometimes we send a wrong or inadequate message. Shawna has just done a great (for her) job of laying down sacrifice bunts in practice, so you say, "Great, that's the way to do it." That's praise. One message that Shawna might get is that she has mastered bunting and has placed a mark at that level for her to perform and on the level that you will accept and expect in the future. She doesn't have to get any better. That's not what you meant her to hear.

So, once in a while we must take one more step, "Great, that was a big improvement. Now, next time you will want to hold off getting into the bunting stance a while longer so that you don't tip off the 3rd baseman too soon." That's encouragement.

Now you have covered all the bases – you have told Shawna that she did something well; you have told her how to improve on this skill; and you have told her that you expect her to attain a higher level of performance.

I observe and evaluate my student teachers four times a semester. At visits #1, #2, and #3, I will most often say, "You did a good job today. Next time I observe you, you'll be a lot better." This is a praise message, an encouragement message, and a positive expectancy message. It also means that I will not accept their present level of performance in future observations.

Praise has to do with your feelings about what is happening now.

Encouragement has to do with how you would like to see it in the future.

Asking the Right Questions

Let's start out with the wrong question: "Lenny, why did you leave your bat over there on the ground?" Answer: (After thinking it over to see if he's about to get into trouble) "I don't know." Not a bad answer and very common. "Why did you . . ." questions are confronting and invite a defensive response.

How about this question: "Lenny, what's the right thing to do with your bat after you take your swings?" "I should put it into the bat rack." "O.K., so will you do that now? Thanks." The neat thing about this is that you are not telling him what to do – he is telling you what he is supposed to do – and then you are having him act on the statement that he just made. Kids have a

Planning for Success

sense of being careful in answering a question dealing with what they were supposed to do so they say, "I don't know." They get practice on this at home from this kind of question: "Lenny, why did you wait until tonight to do that project?" "I don't know" Retry: "Lenny, how could you have handled that assignment the right way?" and Lenny not only knows the answer but he will give it to you – "I should have started it last week."

They get practice at school from this kind of question: "Lenny, why do you have such a messy desk?" "I don't know." (Notice that there is no action to be taken) "Lenny, in what kind of condition should your desk be?" "It should be straightened up." "All right, go ahead and make it that way." (Notice that the correct action has been given to Lenny and now Miss Eastwood can have him act on it.)

Kids know how to do things in the appropriate and right ways. Just ask them the right question.

Okay, dear reader, what do you do when someone says to you, "Why did you...?"

Do You Speak A Foreign Language, Such As Sportsese?

Sometimes coaches in talking to young players will use their sports' terms and even though they don't understand what the coach is saying, the players will nod their heads so they don't look dumb. Using terms that they understand will make the players more secure and able to perform with less stress. You may want to check on whether your players are able to speak up if they don't know what you're talking about or need some clarification.

Good Coaches Stay on the Issue – Not on the Person

Consider this:

Coach Jones: "Jerry, your dumb play cost us that touchdown."

Planning for Success

Coach Jones was dealing with Jerry personally and on his short-comings. He also didn't let him know how to correct his mistake - so that he will be better in the future.

Now consider this:

Coach Smith: "Jerry, it was your job in that defense setup to pick up the tight end."

Coach Smith was dealing with the situation and he told Jerry how to correct the error.

We have to make a distinction between <u>the issue</u> with which we're dealing and <u>the person</u> with whom we're dealing. If we focus on the issue, we're more apt to solve our problem.

The Team's the Thing

"There is no 'I'" in Team." Yes, but there is 'M' and' E' in team. We have all had to deal with that self-centered player who is quick to remind us about the great plays he's made. Direct talk usually doesn't get the job done, so let's come at it from another direction. During some team meetings it's a good idea to talk to your players about how each of them contributes to the team's successes. It is also an opportunity to deal with Billy the Boaster.

Billy made a big interception which helped your team get back into the game and eventually win. He isn't letting anybody forget what he did and how he dragged the team from the jaws of defeat. Let's listen in to Coach Hudson as he deals with this issue:

Who Made That Interception?

Coach: Well, we pulled that one out of the fire. You guys played a great game – you hung in there until we were able to make some breaks. Let's take a look at a real turning point – that interception in the 3rd quarter. Who made that interception?

Everyone looks at Billy who has no trouble smiling - waiting for the accolades.

    Coach: Jeff, what did you do on that play?

Planning for Success

Sandy: I got around my blocker and put some pressure on the quarterback.

Coach: Gary, how about you?

Gary: I shut down the tight end – he never got into his pattern.

Coach: Loren?

Loren: I broke through up the middle and kept the quarterback from stepping up into the pocket.

Coach: Zach?

Zach: Brett and I had the split end covered.

Coach: O.K. and we had the center of the field covered by some of you other backs. O.K., Bobby, where were you?

Bobby: The quarterback got away from Jeff and came my way. I got a piece of his jersey and he pulled away but I was able to get him again.

Coach: Billy?

Billy: The pass was short and wobbly and I stepped in front of the wide receiver and caught the ball.

Coach: And you made a good run back with it. O.K. Let's answer my question now. Who intercepted that pass?

Sam: It sure looks like a lot of guys did a lot of good work.

Coach: That's right. That is what we call teamwork. We all do our job right and good things happen. The real mark of champions is that they all do their job as well as they can and nobody worries about who gets the credit.

The Debriefing Meeting

When is the best time to give your players feedback about the game? Right after the game. Take them out to a quiet place and talk to them about what went well and what needs improving. Those are the only two issues:

1. What went well   and

2. What do we need to work on
next practice?

"I want you to think about the mistakes you made and to decide what you learned from making them, and then I want you to let go of the mistakes and hang on to what you learned. Remember to work on what you learned next practice.

Now, I want you to think about the good plays you made. Close your eyes and replay them in your head. Notice how good they feel. Feel your foot hitting the ball squarely or your follow through on that pass to your team mate or your leaping up and heading that ball away from our goal.

This kind of positive imagery is a strong process that is used by many top athletes. Then give your players a chance to talk about the game, only in positive terms; no complaining, no alibis, no blaming someone else. Any negative statements are followed immediately by "Erase, Erase". The kids catch on this very quickly and jump right in. If any goals have been reached, comment on them. Check the next practice or game scheduled. Thank them for their efforts in the game they just played. Send them home feeling O. K. If they have played a terrible game, this is your opportunity to show some real class. Thank them as you would if they had played their best. Send them home feeling O.K. This is one of the marks of the inspirational coach.

Inquiry Coaching and Interaction

Coach Roach: O. K., Pietro, let's talk about guarding your man awhile. Last game, your man drove around you a couple of times and you got a little frustrated. What was happening and what could you have done?

Planning for Success

Pietro: He was too fast and I didn't have time to react before he got past me.

Coach: Right, so what could you have done about that?

Pietro: I don't know. I was in good position with him when he didn't have the ball but when he got the ball I couldn't stay with him.

Coach: Well, we were playing a tight man-to-man defense and you were really playing in his jersey. What could you have done?

Pietro: I think I see what you're getting to. When he got the ball, I could have moved off of him a little and I would have had more time to react.

Coach: Right, you are pretty quick yourself but you give up that advantage when you try to guard anybody too close. Give yourself a little more space and trust your quick feet. Want to try it out?

Pietro: Yeah, I sure do

Coach: Fran's our quickest driver. Hey, Fran, I want you to play a little one-on-one with Pietro here and I'll even let you have the ball all of the time. O.K., Pietro, check out what you come up with and I'll keep an eye on you for a while.

Pietro: OK, Coach.

Notice: Coach Roach asked him 3 times what he could have done about the problem and led him to a good solution. And then he had him check it out in a real situation.

This is a real incident – I wasn't the coach – If fact, I was the player and John Roach was my junior high school coach.

In this true situation, Coach Roach and I interacted in a very positive way. I got some good information and he had been a good manager and teacher. We worked together.

Some coaches actually feel threatened when a player asks a question or even try to discuss things with them and they are apt to cut him off at the knees. Of course, that's the last time

155

Planning for Success

that player will ask a question and the coach will be heard to say, "These kids never talk to me – they're not even interested enough to ask me what to do if they're not sure how to do it."

The smart Coach knows that his players will learn faster and better if they are involved in the planning and execution of the learning process.

Chapter 5
The Pack/Team Journals

The Coach's Journal

The Player's Journal

The Parents' Journal

The Journals – This set of journals is a tool to help you act positively and actively in improving your work with the kids.

The Team/Coach Agreement – Members of the Pack –
This takes us back to Chapter 1 and to The Wolf and the Pack. Review that material with all of the Coaches. Then send copies of this page and a copy of **The Wolf and the Pack** to the Parents of your Kids. Make this an agenda item in your pre-season meeting with your Parents.

This Agreement has been an essential part of my program – it will prevent a lot of problems down the line.

The Player Profile – Make a copy of this page for each of your players. This information will be used by all of the coaches to get to know each of your players better – to assist you in evaluating each of your players; not from the viewpoint of what's wrong with Sarah, but where is she right now, how can I assist her in her growth as a player and a person, what is her potential?

The Players Rights and Responsibilities is written in the first person singular so that each of your players sees that it refers to him or her. Presentation of this to your players at an early team meeting should be a high priority. It will prevent a lot of problems down the line.

The Parents Files – This section has a page for you to get important information from your parents; including their goals and roles in the project. It also has a pledge for parents to take in terms of their values and roles and their being members of the team. It may help keep things in perspective and also prevent a lot of problems down the line.

NOTE – This journal may be copied for use with your parents and players. Please give credit to the author and book.

Coach's File –To be shared with Parents

The Team/Coach Agreement
Members of the Pack

As the coach or assistant coach I am also a member of the _____ team and a member of The Pack. I must and will work together with my players' parents, the umpires, and the league officials to make this as good an experience as possible for our kids.

In order to do this, I must be as concerned about my own behavior as I am of the behavior of the players.

I understand that the only genuine respect is mutual respect and that I get respect from my players by respecting them.

I understand that the kids are the only persons whose goals and aspirations count in this venture. My own personal goals and aspirations will be met in other ways.

I understand that along with the parents. I am a role model for the behavior of the players, other coaches, and parents and spectators.

I understand that the best environment for the kids to grow personally and to improve their skills must have a minimum of stress, conflict, and disagreement.

I understand that some of the most important lessons that my players are to learn have to do with sportsmanship and good manners.

I understand that one of the major goals of sports is for each participant to have respect for all other participants; including our team players, our opponents, my players' parents, the officials, and other parents.

Signed

_____

Date _____

Coach's File

PLAYER PROFILE

Name_____

Birth Date _____

Address_____

Telephone _____

E-mail_____

Cell _____

Parent(s) _____

Emergency Phone _____

Doctor's Name and Phone Number:
_____

Playing Skills
_____
_____

Personal Qualities, e.g., Leadership, Cooperation, Desire, Confidence, Pride

Personal Goals
_____
_____

Team Goals
_____
_____

Our Plans for working with this Player_____
_____
_____

Player's File – Shared with your Coaches

WHY I WANT TO PLAY

The reasons I want to play this sport are:
_____
_____

This is how I feel about my teammate's
_____
_____

This how I feel about my coaches:
_____
_____

The most successful things I've accomplished in this sport are:
_____
_____

My future successes in this sport will be:
_____
_____

My goals as a Player are:
_____
_____

My goals as a member of the Team are:
_____
_____

My physical conditioning goals are:
_____
_____

My favorite athlete is:
_____

This is what I like and admire about him or her:
_____
_____

Player's Journal – Shared with your Coaches
These are my Rights and Responsibilities. I understand and agree that for every Right that I have, there is a corresponding Responsibility that I must accept and live up to in order to have and keep that Right.

MY RIGHTS

I have the right to be treated fairly.

I have the right to express my ideas and to be listened to.

I have the right to participate in the game as a unique person and athlete.

I have the right to have good coaching.

I have the right to be safe.

I have the right to be treated with respect.

I have the right to have my personal equipment safe and unharmed.

I have the right to share in making the decisions for the team.

I have the right to play and not be 'cut'.

I have the right to be a member of the team.

I have the right to have good equipment.

I have the right not to be embarrassed or insulted.

I HAVE THE RIGHT TO EXPERIENCE THE JOY OF PLAYING
_____.

MY RESPONSIBILITIES

I have the responsibility to treat others fairly.

I have the responsibility to listen to others and consider the worthiness of their ideas.

I have the responsibility to do my best.

I have the responsibility to cooperate with my coach.

I have the responsibility to follow safety rules; and the responsibility not to endanger other people.

I have the responsibility to treat others with respect; this includes teammates, opponents, coaches, and officials.

I have the responsibility to leave other people's equipment alone unless you have their permission.

I have the responsibility to act and think in a responsible manner and to allow others to have their share in the decision-making.

I have the responsibility to attend practices, show up at the game, perform the best I can, and be a constant learner.

I have the responsibility to be a reliable, trustworthy team member.

I have the responsibility to take care of equipment; my own and the team's.

I have the responsibility to not embarrass or insult others.

I HAVE THE RESPONSIBILITY TO MAKE THE BEST OF MY EXPERIENCE.

Coach

_____.

Parent's File – Shared with the Coaches

PARENTS' INVENTORY

Player's Name
_____

My expectations of my Son/Daughter with this team are:
_____
_____

My role in his/her being a player is:
_____
_____

I'm aware of his/her goals with this team and am in Agreement Disagreement with them:
_____

My goals in this venture are In Agreement not in agreement with those of my child:
_____
_____

My expectations of the coach of this team are:
_____
_____

Here are some personal and/or medical concerns about my child:
_____
_____

My reactions to the coach's attitudes and operation are:
_____
_____

Parents' Names
_____

Address_____

Telephone _____

Emergency_____

Doctor's Name and Telephone
_____

Parent's Pledge – For each Parent and shared with the Coach

The Team/Parent Agreement
Members of the Pack

As a parent of I am also a member of the team and a member of the Pack. I must and will work together with the coaches, umpires, and league officials to make this as good an experience as possible for our players. In order to do this, I must be as concerned about my behavior and the behavior of other spectators as I am of the behavior of our players.

I understand that my child is the one and only person in this family whose goals and aspirations count in this venture. My own personal goals and aspirations will be met in other ways.

I understand that along with the coaches and the players I am a role model for the behavior of my child, other players, coaches, and other parents and spectators.

I understand that my child can respond to only one coach at a time – which he/she cannot deal with advice from more than one source at a time.

I understand that the best environment for my child to grow personally and to improve his/her skills must have a minimum of stress, conflict, and disagreement.

I understand that one of the most important lessons that my child is to learn is about sportsmanship and good manners.

I understand that one of the major goals of sports is for each participant to have respect for all other participants; including our team players, opponents, coaches, officials, and other parents.

Therefore, I agree to the following conditions. (Please check the items with which you agree):

I Will:

____1. Support my child totally in his/her venture as a ballplayer.

____2. Support the coaches in their work to make this experience a good one for my child.

____3. Support the umpires and other league officials in their work.

____4. Assist the coaches and league officials in keeping the game as sportsmanlike and enjoyable for the players as possible.

____5. Act as a positive role model for my child, for the other players, and for parents and spectators.

I Will Not:

____1. Use my child to fulfill any of my personal goals.

____2. Use abusive or offensive language toward anyone.

____3. Holler at the umpires - it's the coach's job to argue responsibly.

____4. Make my child or anyone else feel guilty or bad in any way for any reason.

____5. Get on my child for honest errors and mistakes - after all, he/she is just learning how to play the game.

Signature(s)

_____

_____

Comments/Disclaimers

_____

_____

_____

Recommended Books

Sports

Floyd, Raymond	The Elements of Scoring
Gallwey, Tim	The Inner Game of Tennis
	The Inner Game of Golf
Hamm, Mia	Go for the Goal
Jackson, Phil and Hugh, Delehanty	Sacred Hoops
Penick, Harvey	Little Red Book
Rotella, Bob	Golf is Not a Game of Perfect
Shula, Don and Blanchard, Ken	Everyone's a Coach
Sugarman, Karlene	Winning the Mental Way
Thompson, Jim	Shooting in the Dark
Wolff, Rick	Coaching Kids for Dummies
Wooden, Johnny	Wooden: A Lifetime of Observations…

Psychology

Blackerby, Don	Rediscover the Joy of Learning
Dreikurs, Rudolf	Children the Challenge
Dyer, Wayne	What Do You Really Want For Your Children?
Elkind, David	The Hurried Child
Hymes, James	Child Psychology